ANSWERING THE HARD QUESTIONS

ANSWERING THE HARD QUESTIONS

LET IT BE *the* END *of a* CHAPTER, NOT *the* END *of the* BOOK

DEVIN FISH

ANSWERING THE HARD QUESTIONS
Let It Be the End of a Chapter, Not the End of the Book

FIRST EDITION

ISBN   978-1-5445-5167-8   *Hardcover*
        978-1-5445-5166-1   *Paperback*
        978-1-5445-5168-5   *Ebook*

CONTENTS

CHAPTER BREAKDOWN 9

1. LET IT BE THE END OF A CHAPTER,
   NOT THE END OF THE BOOK 19

2. THE HARD QUESTIONS 33

3. RESTORING FAITH 49

4. THE POWER OF THE MIND 61

5. FINDING YOUR PURPOSE 75

6. ACTIONS REQUIRED 89

7. THE TEST 103

8. REBUILDING YOUR CONFIDENCE 125

9. EVERYONE STRUGGLES 141

10. FINDING YOUR VOICE 165

11. CREATING A NEW CHARACTER 179

12. THE COST 191

13. THE FINAL TEST 199

14. THE CLOSING 207

    THE QUESTIONS 211

CHAPTER BREAKDOWN

CHAPTER 1: LET IT BE THE END OF A CHAPTER, NOT THE END OF THE BOOK

Before you can understand the beliefs I hold today, you first need to see the story that shaped them.

- **Before You Begin to Read:** A warning to the reader: You must be honest and accountable. This book asks questions only you can answer.
- **My Story**
- **My First Three Philosophies:** The first step toward change.
- **Ask Yourself the Hard Questions:** Dig deeper. These aren't easy questions, but they lead to real answers.
- **Tell Your Story:** Now that you've read my story, tell your own.
- **The Most Important Lesson a Parent Can Teach You:** You learned lessons not just from what your parents said but also from what they failed to do. Even flawed love can leave behind wisdom.

- **Speak Up:** Take courage and action with this challenge and warning.

CHAPTER 2: THE HARD QUESTIONS

Before you begin, we need to know where you are.

- **A Call for Help**
- **The Equation:** Changing your life is like solving a math problem—once you figure out one piece, the next one becomes easier.
- **It Only Takes One Question:** One question, the seed of transformation, is all it takes to change your direction.
- **Complete Honesty:** Honesty is the foundation of change. Without it, your answers will only lead you in circles.
- **Why I Chose to Live:** Gather the courage to answer the ultimate question of life and death.
- **Vulnerability:** Let your guard down. While honesty takes an emotional toll, it also grants you power.
- **Why I Wrote This Book:** Tie your questions to the beginning of purpose, a reason to speak and guide others.

CHAPTER 3: RESTORING FAITH

We must first restore what you have forgotten before we can start over.

- **Going to War with God**
- **Finding Faith:** This is a reflection on how faith, once resisted, became my foundation for meaning. I acknowledge my early conflict with belief and how suffering, doubt, and introspection led to new spiritual depth.

- **When You Have Nothing:** What do you cling to when your perceived identity is stripped away?
- **Why Do You Need to Believe in Something?:** A life without belief leaves you vulnerable.
- **What Is Stronger—Faith or Hope?:** Faith acts while hope waits, a powerful contrast between two forces often confused.
- **Do You Believe in Free Will?:** I examine control, responsibility, and whether we are the heroes or villains of our own lives.
- **What If Everyone Was Perfect?:** I challenge our ideas of fairness, purpose, and flawlessness—and whether perfection would eliminate the point of living.
- **My Biggest Struggles with Faith:** This is an honest confession of doubt. I wrestle with belief when reality seems harsh, but finding purpose has become my bridge to belief.

CHAPTER 4: THE POWER OF THE MIND

The mind is what lost faith, so now we must rebuild our thoughts.

- **A Glimpse into Hell**
- **You Can Make Yourself Depressed:** Belief alone can shape our emotional state, and the same mechanism can be used to choose joy.
- **What Do You Say to Yourself?:** Your inner dialogue either builds or destroys you, and you can come to recognize the old self who no longer belongs.
- **Do I Regret Some of the Decisions I Made at That Time?:** Own your past. View regret as a teacher, not a curse. Your lowest points can become your beginning.
- **Think Independently:** Practice mental sovereignty. Free

yourself from outside influence and take full ownership of your beliefs and mindset.

- **Do You Always Need to Apply All the Lessons?:** Understand when to apply what you've learned and when to move on from a lesson that's served its purpose.

CHAPTER 5: FINDING YOUR PURPOSE

Now that you have regained your thoughts, it's time to choose a direction.

- **When All Is Lost, Something Is Found**
- **What Is My Role?:** Clarify your position in life. Step into responsibility and meaning.
- **Is Motivation Necessary?:** In your purpose, you will find the motivation.
- **After I Decided to Live:** This is a personal account of taking first steps–pursuing service, facing failure, and finding a path forward.
- **Fueling the Flame:** Identify what drives you. What do you long for deep inside, and are you willing to fight for it?
- **What If I Don't Deserve What I Desire?:** Confront the doubt that blocks progress. Move past feelings of unworthiness.
- **Look for Opportunity:** Seek the right audience or mentors. The timing may not be perfect, but the chance could still be right.
- **Journey of the Goal:** The beginning is the hardest part, but the journey shapes who you become. From battling inner demons to becoming the hero, your goal is the story, not just the destination.

CHAPTER 6: ACTIONS REQUIRED

The perfect time to start will never come because that time is right now.

- **A Necessary Sacrifice**
- **Why Should You Act Now?:** Don't wait for the perfect moment, because someone out there might not have another chance.
- **What Makes Someone Successful?:** Success often stems from consistency and clarity, not just passion or timing.
- **Do I Believe in the Grind Mindset?:** Grinding without sharpening your skills leaves you dull. Know when to push and when to pause.
- **Create a Team:** Building a council of inspiration and guidance strengthens your path forward.
- **Be Patient, Listen, and Observe:** Not every moment is the right moment; learn to wait, prepare, and strike when it's your time.
- **Protect Your Dreams:** Don't give your dreams to those who will tear them down. Some desires must be guarded until the right time.

CHAPTER 7: THE TEST

No trial is complete without obstacles blocking the way.

- **Repeated Temptations**
- **What You Don't Always Need:** What you have at the start is not important. It's about taking the next step.
- **Quit Predicting the Future:** Live in the present; the future has yet to come.
- **Are You Ready?:** Prepare for the unknown by finding read-

iness through action, not perfection. You have to take the small wins before you achieve a big victory.

- **You Will Be Tested:** Challenges are inevitable, and your beliefs, mindset, and discipline will all wade through fire.
- **Redefine Failure:** Failure is not the end. It may be necessary progress in disguise.
- **Is Failure Bad?:** Let's take an honest look at how failure shapes growth and whether it's truly a negative.
- **How Much Does Luck Play a Factor in the Story?:** I explore the balance between effort, timing, and the uncontrollable role of luck.
- **Broken:** Experience shattered me, yet I discovered unexpected gifts through the pain.

CHAPTER 8: REBUILDING YOUR CONFIDENCE

Broken by others, you are restored through belief in yourself.

- **Finding Self-love**
- **Why Must People Fall?:** Sometimes suffering is not a punishment but a foundation for someone else's rise.
- **Fear of Rejection:** Rejection can lead you to the path you're supposed to be on.
- **How to Overcome Fear:** Let fear guide you; do not let it control you.
- **Body, Spirit, and Mind:** True confidence is built from the balance and alignment of your full being.
- **The Most Important Person in Your Life Should Be You:** If you don't value yourself first, you'll always rely on others to define your worth.

CHAPTER 9: EVERYONE STRUGGLES

Opposition fights for control of your life.

- **Rising Instability**
- **What Got Me Through the Hard Years:** Solitude, discipline, and purpose—the foundation of enduring pain—helped me persevere through the struggle.
- **My Biggest Struggle:** This internal battle nearly broke me, but this question saved me.
- **Learn Your Cycles:** Recognize the loops of pain before they repeat.
- **When to Move On:** Know when to stop enduring and start walking away.
- **Forgive But Don't Forget:** Healing isn't forgetting—it's remembering without letting the memory of the pain control you.
- **The Sandstorm:** Sacrifice comfort for gains.

CHAPTER 10: FINDING YOUR VOICE

Silence is no longer an option.

- **Lost in Silence**
- **Sharing, Giving, Parasites, and Thieves:** Let's reflect on generosity, boundaries, and the danger of those who take advantage of kindness.
- **Final Thoughts on Scamming:** I vulnerably admit my most painful regret: being scammed out of free will. I moved forward with accountability, emotional truth, and a quiet transition toward healing.
- **My Best Day:** Your worst days will turn into the greatest victories.

- **The Puzzle:** Putting yourself back together.
- **Remember Where You Came From:** As you start to put yourself back together, remember what it was like to be in your shoes.
- **Find Yourself:** Find yourself, and you will find your voice.

CHAPTER 11: CREATING A NEW CHARACTER

The struggles are not over yet, but you must still walk the path.

- **A Need for Change**
- **Why You Should Want to Change:** You must recognize the necessity of transformation before growth can occur.
- **Choose to Live:** Choosing to live is the foundation for every next step.
- **Why You Feel Lost:** Confusion often precedes clarity–it's part of transformation.
- **Who Do You Want to Be?:** Define your ideal self, based on your own truth–not others' expectations.
- **The Path to Follow:** Once identity is chosen, direction becomes the next step.
- **The Other Path:** Alternative routes may offer the most authentic way forward.
- **What If...?:** Consider risk, possibility, and how unknowns can guide us.
- **Why Did It Take So Long to Write This Book?:** I take responsibility for my transformation and the death of the old self.

CHAPTER 12: THE COST

You can start over, but are you willing to pay the price?

- **A Final Destination**
- **What Trophy Do You Want?:** What are you chasing? Is it worth the sacrifice?
- **Every Gift Comes with a Curse:** Our strengths often come with hidden burdens.
- **Cost vs. Worth:** There are trade-offs between effort and what we gain in return.
- **The Average Lifespan:** Time is currency. How we spend it matters.
- **Sacrifice the Present:** Meaningful change means giving up comfort now for something greater later.
- **Obstacles Come with Reward:** Challenges come with hidden rewards—growth, skill, and impact. The greater the cost, the greater the potential return.

CHAPTER 13: THE FINAL TEST

Work in the darkness; shine in the light.

- **Let It Be the End of a Chapter, Not the End of the Book**
- **Death:** Mortality reminds us of life's urgency and value.
- **Why Do We Suffer?:** Pain has purpose: reveal, test, and teach.
- **The Darkness:** The truest parts of ourselves shine in the darkness.
- **The Purpose of Light and Darkness:** Contrast is what gives direction, clarity, and meaning.
- **Two Wishes:** Our desires reveal our truth and values.
- **Look Up, Not Down:** Rise, even in the wake of darkness.
- **A New Wish:** This is a wish for my readers.

CHAPTER 14: THE CLOSING

All good stories must come to an end. But yours is just beginning.

- **How This Book Was Made:** I focused on belief and made the biography afterward.
- **One Day:** Take the time to appreciate the present day.
- **The Golden Touch:** You were never broken; you just needed to see that truth for yourself.
- **The Speech:** Step fully into your purpose and share it with the world.
- **The Door:** The final threshold: Will you walk through it or stay behind?
- **The End of the Story:** It is the last page—but the beginning of your journey.

THE QUESTIONS: YOUR STORY BEGINS HERE.

LET IT BE THE END OF A CHAPTER, NOT THE END OF THE BOOK

Before you can understand the beliefs I hold today, you first need to see the story that shaped them.

BEFORE YOU BEGIN TO READ

This isn't just a book; it's a challenge. I answer many questions in this book, but there are just as many you'll have to answer on your own. As a reader, it is your responsibility to answer questions with complete honesty. I cannot do that for you.

By accepting this challenge, you are making a promise not to me but to yourself. I can't judge or help someone who is not in front of me. I can't teach someone who is not willing to learn. I can't change someone who does not want to change. The one person whose judgment you can't escape, however, is your own. *There is no distance you can travel that will allow you to run away from yourself.*

People often misunderstand what it means to change your mind. It doesn't permanently fix you. Instead, you develop a powerful mindset that can shut down negative thoughts. But those negative thoughts don't just disappear. They will come back to test you. I became aware early in my childhood that those negative thoughts consumed me.

It took me until my mid-twenties to confront them. Some of the negative events I discuss in this story still haunt me to this day. The difference now lies in how I view them. I learned valuable lessons from each of those experiences. I am about to share with you the darkest moments of my life, both circumstantial and self-inflicted. Death, addiction, and immoral decisions will not be off the table. *While I do not glorify my actions, I also will not hide them.*

My name is Devin Fish. I was born on July 19, 1997, in Rockford, Illinois. I grew up in Rockford, but I only go back about once a year to see my family. I recommend you keep driving through Illinois, because there isn't much to see in Rockford besides a rundown city rife with crime. At eighteen, I joined the Army to get away from my hometown. Oddly enough, it has been said that fighting in wars is safer than living in my hometown.

To give you an idea, Rockford's crime rate exceeds both the state and national averages. Yes, if you compare it to populous places like Chicago, then the rates appear inconsequential. But if you scale the rates down to Rockford's size, both cities are rated 5 out of 100 on the crime index, meaning that 95 percent of the United States is safer than Rockford.

I spent my childhood there—the first eighteen years of my life—until the summer of 2016. While I stayed in that city, I moved about sixteen times before joining the Army. The average person in the United States will move only twelve times in their lifetime. I lived in a house, a farm, a trailer park, an apartment, and even a motel. Different people housed me, including my mother, father, grandmother, two aunts, and my mother's friends. I had run away from one of those homes and then refused to stay with my father during one of those times.

My living conditions were mostly poor. There were times when I did not have hot water, air conditioning in the summer, or even—for a short stint—a toilet. We survived on food stamps. When comparing myself to others, I could clearly see that my family and its support system were poor. I didn't have internet or cable at home until I was in high school. The best thing we had was Fox Channel 39, where I found some entertainment. My friends at school had smartphones and iPods, while I had a CD player and a flip phone.

I attended seven schools during my childhood, and I returned to some of them multiple times. I was a shy kid, on the small side, with the last name Fish, so I was easily bullied by the other kids. I have heard just about every fish joke you can think of by now. In school, I was practically mute; if I didn't know you, I wouldn't talk to you. I refused to work on school projects to avoid talking to anyone. Looking back now, I realize this led to many issues in the future, isolating me from the real world.

I understood the class material fine, but the problem was, at an early age, I developed a mindset of not caring for life in general. While I passed my classes, my father would occasionally get a phone call from my school saying I was missing assignments—sometimes in the double digits, up to fifty at a time. I was not off to an excellent start in life. I had already given up. My family is still surprised by how I turned out based on my unconventional upbringing. Sometimes, so am I.

To give you an idea of how my life went, I will tell you three stories about my father, my mother, and me that happened over the course of a couple of years.

***

The first story took place in 2016. In my last semester of high school, I was preparing to leave for the Army. I lived with my father at the time, who struggled through some stressful situations. We lived in an apartment, and I had just gotten back from school. As the bus pulled up outside our apartment, I found it swarmed with police cars. Broken glass peppered the sidewalk, and our smashed air conditioning unit lay lifeless on the ground.

I paused for a couple of seconds while my heartbeat started to race. It was one of those gut feelings you get before you know you're about to have a bad day. As my heart sank in my chest, I approached and asked myself, "Is this really happening?"

The police officer then confirmed my suspicions. He asked me which apartment I stayed in, and after I told him, he escorted me to my aunt's place, who lived a couple of miles down the road. After they spoke with her, she told me that my father was in the hospital.

He had resisted arrest and was taken down by force, tased, and sedated. He had combined Fireball Whisky and cocaine, which led to explosive behavior. Eventually, my aunt and I went to the hospital to check on him. He tried to look away, ashamed that his family had to see him in this condition. That his son had to look at him, handcuffed to the bedrail at a hospital, his arms covered in cuts.

Later that day, I retrieved my belongings from the apartment, or what was left of it. Mostly, I grabbed my clothes. Everything else in that apartment had been destroyed by my father. It was a gruesome image; without context, you would have thought someone had just been murdered.

His blood was everywhere—on the walls, furniture, and even the ceiling. Everything that could be broken had been—a glass table, TVs, mirrors, a laptop, and cabinets. Even the AC unit, which can weigh more than a hundred pounds and is secured to the wall, got thrown through the window. After all this happened, I still had to go to back to school the next day.

* * *

The second story is about my mother, who raised me when I was younger but eventually had to give me up because she couldn't afford to keep me. She sent me off to live with my grandmother. I would visit my mom on the weekends, which was easy enough since she just lived a couple of blocks down the road. However, her living conditions were extremely poor, and I often avoided spending time there.

The biggest issue that made me not want to stay over was that she was a heavy smoker, so the entire place reeked of cigarettes. The second was that she had developed an addiction to pain medications. She would regularly take them, sell them, and buy them. Once, during a conversation she and I were having, she passed out, mid-sentence. When that happened, I quietly walked out the door and left. She hadn't been my mother for quite some time. She was a shell of her former self, a zombie. Her body was present, but her mind was gone.

She experienced so much trauma and grief in her life, so I understand her, and sometimes I do not blame her. She had to give up both of her kids, go without a vehicle or money, and drop out of school. She lost her mother the previous year. My mother never lived with my father, so I was exposed to both of their worlds simultaneously. My mom's addiction had been active long before the incident I described with my father.

However, the closer I got to departing for the military, the better she seemed to be. By the time I got back from Basic

Training, everything was back to normal. She had a vehicle and a job; life was looking better for her. Sometimes, I think that maybe she did it to make sure I came back.

Shortly after that, I was stationed at Fort Hood, Texas, and started the day at base reception, preparing to head to my new unit. That night, I was with a couple of friends when my mother called me. We talked for a couple of minutes and then said our goodbyes. I didn't realize that it would be the last time I'd get to speak to her.

The next day, I got a Red Cross message saying that she was in the hospital. Once I arrived and spoke with her medical providers, they explained that she'd had a bad reaction to medication. It had fried her brain.

As the oldest son, I had to make a tough decision: keep her on life support and hope she would recover, or let her go. I decided to let her go; I based that difficult choice on her religious practices. However, I learned a few minutes after making the decision that it didn't matter anyway. A nurse delivered the news that there was nothing they could do; they had to take her off the life support, whether we liked it or not. I watched as my mom's heart rate turned into a straight line on the monitor. It was July 9, 2017, a couple of days before my birthday.

I often wonder how addiction starts. Some people start using out of curiosity; some chase the high; others want the thrill. What is the difference between the person who does it for fun and the person who can't stop? For the person who can't stop, I imagine they are trying to run away from the world they created or were forced to live in. If you live a good life, you don't depend on a substance to keep you going. *Addiction is an escape from reality that often comes at the cost of life.*

* * *

Then, of course, to keep the family tradition going, I found myself in the hospital in 2019. Neither drugs nor alcohol put me there; I willingly admitted myself. I recognized that I had a problem and that I would not survive much longer. Why might that be, you ask? Well, part of it I have already told you: From an early age, I didn't care, and that was true until I was twenty-two.

I was a pretty pessimistic person. I thought everything was bad, the world was out to get me, and that I was a big loser. I hated my job, I hated the Army, I hated the world. Most importantly, I hated myself. While the incidents with my parents happened as a teenager, my rising instability started in elementary school. When you stop caring about your life for more than ten years, it does a number on your mind.

If you don't care about your life, you start to look for care in different places. So, I looked to others for approval—real or fake—anyone who would give it to me. I always felt alone, so I looked at dating apps, which is where my troubles began in this third story. I tried every dating app, from the good to the bad, the popular to the obscure, seeking the companionship I couldn't find within myself. The problem was that I never found anyone genuine; they were all scammers who wanted my money or something else from me.

Even when I knew someone was a scammer, I would still give in to them because I didn't want to be alone. I fraternized with scammers for about a year straight. During that time, I zeroed out my bank account more than once, I had my social media accounts leaked, and, on several occasions, I was blackmailed. Despite all of this, I continued. I was so desperate that I didn't care what anyone did to me. If you don't care about your life, then what difference does it make, right? My morals were out the window at this point. I went from not caring about life to something even lower.

As I did many times before, I went back to a dating website and got a match. The person's profile picture looked pretty average, and they said they were eighteen years old. By that statement alone, you probably know what came next. We started a conversation. One thing led to another, and the user admitted they were only sixteen or seventeen. I can't remember which. Maybe part of me doesn't want to. But I didn't stop messaging them, even though every ounce of my body told me I should. I gave them exactly what they wanted. The next morning, everything went down.

I got a call from a man claiming to be the person's father. He confronted me and said the person had gone to the hospital. I tried to deny everything, but I knew he had me. That experience changed my life. I realized that with one bad decision, I could have lost everything, including my life. I paid them everything they asked for, multiple times.

I never found an answer as to whether it was a real person or a great scam. Part of me still wonders, but I have made peace with both possibilities. The police were never involved, and no reports were filed. My only insight that this was a scam came later; at the time, it felt very real, and I saw my life flash before my eyes.

During that time frame, I considered ways to take my own life, and those thoughts continued for a couple of months. That experience sent me to the hospital. (The lessons I learned in the hospital will be shared later in this book.) Afterward, I started to make my recovery. While I still struggled with my self-worth and being alone, I became adept at detecting scams.

It has now been six years since the night on which I nearly took my life—and believe me, changing a mindset that I nurtured for over ten years was no easy switch.

MY FIRST THREE PHILOSOPHIES

I learned several lessons along the way, and they culminate in this book. I learned to develop a philosophy to aid my progress in changing how I think and how I view the world. My core philosophy has three parts; over time, though, I have created about forty insights to express how I approach my daily life. By the time I am done, I imagine there will be double, if not triple, that amount. But the three most important to me are the ones I have kept with me for many years—ones I have used as a foundation upon which to build all the others.

Philosophy Part 1: Everything happens for a reason. This provides purpose for events in life that we do not understand or questions we do not have the answers to yet. The stories I told you were terrible, and I hope no one else has to go through those experiences. But they were some of the most defining moments of my life.

The first story I told about my father is the reason I do not drink; the second story about my mother is the reason I do not smoke or rely on prescription drugs. My father is now five years sober and drug-free. I still find it fascinating how some of the worst moments of our lives can change us for the better.

Maybe without that moment in the apartment, my father would have kept drinking; and perhaps if he had continued, he would not be here today. While my mother was not given a second chance, her death also taught me a valuable lesson: to appreciate the time we have, as we never know when our last moments will come. I have also passed that lesson on to others in their time of need.

Philosophy Part 2: Accept what has happened. Sometimes, life hits you like a freight train, and you ask yourself, "Did that really happen?" If you answered yes to your own question, then congrats, you have already accomplished this step. No matter how good or bad something is, there is no point in pretending something did not happen. The more you avoid a memory, the more it festers—I promise you that. Take accountability for what happened to you, even if the initial circumstance was out of your control. *Nothing in your past can be changed. We live in the present, not the past.*

Philosophy Part 3: Move on. This is where most people give up. When we do not move on, a part of us gets stuck in the past. When that happens, we relive those moments of our life repeatedly, preventing us from taking purposeful action. So, I ask you this question: *If you are stuck in the past, what will make the future any different?*

ASK YOURSELF HARD QUESTIONS

Asking yourself easy questions leads to easy answers. Ask yourself the hard questions. If you don't like who you are, then you can't continue with the same answers as before. In order to change, you must come up with new solutions.

You must ask more complex questions to come up with those better answers. An easy question would be, *Am I happy?* It's a simple, yes-or-no question. A deeper, open-ended question would then be, *What would make me happy?* Maybe the answer to that question comes easily to you. But people who haven't felt happy in years will struggle to answer it. The hard questions should make you think, make you ask more questions, and at times, make you uncomfortable.

You see, when you ask the hard questions, you will unlock information stored away in the back of your mind. Maybe when you were young, you had grand ambitions, but the world fought back. *You set aside what you wanted in life and became someone else. The problem is that the person you created will never be you.*

At the beginning of each chapter, I'll share personal stories and my thoughts. At the end of each section, I'll pose a reflection question. There is also a section at the end of the book (The Questions) where you can write your answers. I want you to think about what your one question is before reading the reflection questions. Start to ask yourself the hard questions now, so that by the time I ask you some, you are already thinking about your answers.

Let's start with the most challenging question I can ask you.

TELL YOUR STORY

One of the most essential parts of your journey is telling your story. In fact, I believe it is irresponsible not to tell your story to others. Stories give people hope when they can find none left in themselves. A story, whether complex or straightforward, sheds light in the darkness. I tell my story to help others avoid my mistakes.

No matter what I or you do, that won't stop the same mistakes from happening. Some people have to learn the hard way. They will need to live out their own mistakes to learn their lessons. I learned my lesson in 2019; others are still learning. I find my courage to keep going not for me, but for the ones who still need to hear the story. *If someone is in that dark place right now, the difference in surviving another day could be knowing that someone else found the light in their darkest days.*

THE MOST IMPORTANT LESSON A PARENT CAN TEACH

While I love my parents, they each came with their flaws, as you have already read. But both of them taught me valuable lessons. My father taught me the most valuable lesson a parent can teach their children to help them succeed in the world.

My father always used to say, "Do what I say, not what I do." I used to hate that. In my mind, I thought, *You're just trying to control me and saying I'm a child.* It wasn't until later in life that I knew what this meant. It had nothing to do with control. It had everything to do with my father trying to protect me from making the same mistakes he'd made in his life.

One of the things my dad used to do was pick on me, push me around, and play-fight with me. He would get me going, sometimes to the point where I started screaming at him. When I got old enough to hit back, he stopped doing that. But a couple of years later, he told me the reason behind his actions. He already knew that life wouldn't be kind to me. Our last name was Fish, and I was a small, quiet kid on top of that.

So, any chance he got, he would make me uncomfortable or make me face my fears. But he did it out of love. He wasn't trying to hurt me; he wanted to give me the strength to make it in a world that didn't always have the best intentions. So, what was the lesson he taught me? *The greatest teachers are not the ones who get it right, but the ones who show us what not to do—and love us enough to warn us anyway.*

SPEAK UP

Why do you need to speak up? To be heard.

For over fifteen years, I hid my story from the world. In that shame-filled silence, I found most of my problems—so much knowledge held back for those who needed it more than I.

The darkness gains its power in silence. It blinds you with fear and traps you in doubt.

But the truth is, if you speak, you will be heard. If you lose, you will learn. If you are silent, it will never happen.

Silent on the dreams that never came true.

Silent on the books you never wrote.

Silent on the songs you never sang.

Silent on the best experiences waiting for you that will never happen.

Instead of staying silent, speak up for what you believe in; someone out there is waiting to listen.

But be aware: Silence will always be waiting for its next guest to stay forever...and always.

CHAPTER 2

THE HARD QUESTIONS

Before you begin, we need to know who you are.

A CALL FOR HELP

I only had two options: life or death. There was no in-between when I admitted myself to the hospital. I had to make that decision before accepting help. There wasn't any time left to push back what I had built up inside of me. This wasn't just a simple overnight fix; this issue had been boiling in my head for years.

That decision to accept help is where this book first began to take root, not on paper but in my mind. It was on the worst days of my life that I realized I wasn't alone. But even back then, I never told anyone what was really causing my issues. I still couldn't be honest with myself at that point. I was still hiding.

My military career wasn't going exactly as planned, either, which didn't help my circumstances. I initially signed a six-year contract to become a nurse. They offered a license to anyone who could pass the course. But what they didn't always make clear was that they cram three years of schooling into one year. That also came with a 70 percent dropout rate.

Before you get to school, you first must pass Basic Training. For me, that training was in Fort Leonard Wood, Missouri. I had failed my first go-round due to rifle marksmanship, missing by one shot. When that happened, I got recycled to the next unit and had to undergo corrective training.

This may not seem bad to most people who have never experienced military life. But I can assure you that waking up before the sun, getting yelled at throughout the day, and then physically paying for it later isn't easy. This also happened during midsummer in Missouri; the heat was on a scale all its own.

Within the first day of training, we had heat casualties; one Soldier was so bad off that we had to send him home. I stayed on the third floor for basic, but if someone opened the door on the *first floor* to go outside, we immediately felt the heat. When we did corrective training on the hot cement, it could burn the skin off our hands—which is why we had to do it inside for most of the cycle. I unfortunately made it harder on myself within the first week of being there.

I tripped one day while marching and ended up scraping skin off my hand right below the thumb, where the circular part of the meat is. The skin was gone entirely, and corrective training typically involved push-ups. So anytime that happened, I put the skinless part of my hand on the ground, pushing off the scalding-hot cement. Being on the concrete, little pieces of rubble and rocks would get into my wound, and I would have to pull them out, hoping for my injury to heal eventually. I added another four to six weeks of misery to my sentence by missing that one shot.

Before they recycled me, though, our senior Drill Sergeant sat me down in his office. The first thing he wanted me to know was that on day one of Basic Training, he saw me. He didn't think I'd make it past day one, and he said, "Yet here you are, four weeks in." Eventually, he reassured me that I would do just fine and make it through next time. He was right. I passed my next cycle.

While the environment is more relaxed in AIT (Advanced Individual Training) for nursing school, it is still within the Army. So even then, you are on a set schedule. You wake up before the sun rises, hope not to get yelled at, and then it's death by PowerPoint for up to seven hours a day. I went on to fail nursing school only a couple of weeks into the course. The mental demand and some emotional issues I was going through led to a quick downfall.

Once you fail, you become a holdover, which is even worse. You keep the same schedule, only instead of going to school, you sit on a bench all day until your next assignment. The worst part was that it was fall, so shivering on a metal bench was an everyday experience, for multiple hours a day. I sat there for numerous months waiting for my next assignment. I eventually got my next class, which was to become a Calvary Scout. But here's the thing about being a scout: their training is linked to Basic Training.

For the third time, I had to go back to Basic Training. I was going backward before my career had even started. In AIT, you have some freedom. After school is done, you can have a phone and at least explore. But in Basic Training, you have nothing. Your schedule is made to a tee for each hour. You will eat, train, and sleep when they tell you—no sooner, no later. They like to keep you on your toes, too.

The Drill Sergeants at Fort Benning upped the ante compared to my previous cycles. When we got comfortable, they would toss our bay area. At the start, it would take us an hour to clean it up, but by the end, we had it down to about twenty minutes. If they were feeling really sadistic that day, they would fill mop buckets with water to toss around or even grab sauce packets from the dining area to tear open and spread across our bay.

But the worst day I ever saw was when one of the senior Drill Sergeants returned from training. I remember that they would talk about how strict he was, but I still didn't see this next part coming. When he got back, all hell broke loose. He "smoked" the entire company for a couple of hours.

I imagine they called it "smoked" because it caused the body to become so hot that you could see literal steam coming off it by the time you were done. But he didn't stop there. When we thought it was over, it was only just beginning. He put everyone on a track and told us to run until he said to stop. I put two and two together quickly; he wanted to see maximum effort.

He was trying to see who was willing to push themselves and who was holding back. So, when he blew a whistle to run, I sprinted nearly a quarter mile. I earned my way off the track within a couple of minutes, but for the rest of my team members, not so much. Some of them stayed on that track for hours until he was satisfied. The next day, half a company of Soldiers went to sick call to get checked out for injury.

As you can probably guess, they later investigated that Drill Sergeant. He changed his tactics. If he couldn't make us pay physically, he would take the only thing we had left: time. He would put us in a position of attention, with our bodies straight, hands at our sides, and eyes forward. He would then leave us there for a couple of hours, standing in our own silence.

Most people only go through this experience for ten weeks, plus the length of their AIT. But I must have set a new record—I was in and out of this training environment for about a year.

Just one of my many stories on how life should have won, but for some reason, I kept going.

My life didn't get any easier, as you know; once I made it out of training, I headed to my first unit at Fort Hood, Texas. To give you a recap, before leaving for Basic Training, I saw my father in the hospital, covered in blood. Then, after being kicked around by the military for a year, my mother's passing happened a couple of weeks later.

During the time of my mother's death, I had no money. I broke my debit card, so it was not functional at the time. Luckily, the Army has a program called Army Emergency Relief, which charges no interest for giving financial help in these types of circumstances.

As for being a scout, I didn't mind it at first. Once I got back to Fort Hood, I traveled to South Korea in Camp Humphries to join my platoon. At the time, it felt more like a family, and even though I was the new person, I still felt welcomed. I spent a couple of months in Korea before we returned to Fort Hood.

But my time of enjoying being a scout was short-lived. Once we got back, we were put on a three-month detail at Fort Knox called the Cadet Summer Training Program. Once again, I was in an extremely hot and humid environment. Think of the training program for future officers before they join the Army. However, they received special treatment compared to what the enlisted went through.

While they were training, we handled everything else for them. We set up their ranges, handled their ammunition, provided transportation, and even did their laundry while in the field. We referred to the worst of the details as tent city. While everyone was assigned their own detail, this one they pulled from every group to help. The tents were there to provide cover for the Cadets in case of a storm.

Each tent took about an hour to put up with a crew of about twenty people. We called it tent city because there were about one hundred tents to set up, each holding about fifty people. This was a weeklong detail. At one point, after half the tents were set up, the Cadets decided they were not satisfied with how they looked. They decided that the tents would have to move.

All of this was in midsummer, at around ninety to one hundred degrees, the entirety of the detail. The Soldiers slaved away day by day for the Cadets, not even in the Army yet. Those tents would also have to be torn down before we left. The worst part is that they didn't even use them once.

Then there was my actual detail: ammunition. We had to receive it from a holding area, count it, store it, and take it out to the ranges. This was a twenty-four-hour detail, meaning we had to take twenty-four-hour shifts while also supporting it. We had two different holding areas, which made it worse. Once the Cadets were done, we then had to pick them up, sort them, and count once again.

The problem was that the Cadets didn't care about the mess. They would mix the ammunition with live and unused rounds. Then we would sort the ammo into live and unused rounds. This task once took us five or six hours. Once we sorted it, it had to be taken back to the official holding area for turn-in. If you can guess, we would then have to sort it once again for them.

The worst part of the experience was that, while we were sorting, they found too many live rounds and sent us back. All that hard work down the drain—another five hours of sorting and turn-in would follow. The days of a twenty-four-hour guard were not great, either. It turns out that counting in the Army can be hard.

As mentioned before, we had to keep a count of all the

rounds, and we used a spreadsheet to display the numbers. During this detail, we were responsible for over a million rounds of ammunition. Each type was sorted in boxes weighing between twenty and fifty pounds. We had containers stacked with each of those boxes, which helped keep the count.

But on almost every shift, it seemed someone forgets how to count. When that happened, we would have to take out all the boxes and figure out where the issue was. It would sometimes take hours to recount all the boxes. Every shift, we had to do a transfer, which was when we found out how bad our day was going to be.

I can't begin to tell you how enraged I was throughout this detail. It's one thing to write about it, but living it for ninety days is an entirely different experience. Imagine being stuck in Basic Training environments for over a year, doing everything yourself and with your team. Then, to come out of that, only to have to hand walk people who are not even in the Army yet. A lot of my rage for the Army was built up during those ninety days. It wasn't the treatment of Basic Training that got me; it was seeing others given different privileges.

The detail was eventually over, and we returned to Fort Hood, but I still carried the rage within me. I didn't show it in person, but I let it out when no one was watching. By the time we got back, everything had changed. There was new leadership. There were also new sections and Soldiers. The problem was that some of the people who had been with the unit for years had also left.

It no longer felt like family, but instead a divide, and people wanted it to go back to what it was. The previous leadership kept people in check. With the new leadership, it almost felt like each section was on its own. Some would be working while others were never to be seen. Unfortunately, by the time one of the leaders stepped up to help me, it was too late. The rage I had found in the summer leaked not only into my job as a scout but also into the Army as a whole.

It only became worse when I didn't know my job and was thrown into leadership positions. There was nothing about being a scout that I enjoyed. A scout is the eyes and ears of the commander to help make battlefield decisions. It's a combat-related job that requires frequent field events and demands a certain mentality toward Soldiers—a mentality akin to that of the Drill Sergeants from Basic Training.

You had to be strict, knowing that it could cost someone's life. You showed little to no remorse during corrective training. Being nice wasn't always an option. But stemming back to childhood, yelling at people or even punishing them was never my style. I also knew that I could get very nasty if left unchecked. I could see that toxic personality in others at the time, and I didn't want to turn into that kind of person.

I hated being a scout with a passion. I even told myself repeatedly that if I stayed a scout, I was getting out. I signed up to help people and save lives. I didn't have that combat personality, which didn't help my self-esteem or confidence. Tell a fish to climb a tree, and it will fail. I'm an indoor person who is quiet, likes to help people, doesn't shoot well, and is nearly blind in one eye. None of that meshed well with what being a good scout required.

Combine the hatred I had for the Army and my job as a scout, and it was enough to send me over the edge. But to throw in the fact that my personal life was in shambles as well, from all the blackmail I was enduring, would ultimately be too much to handle.

I was able to keep it under control for a very long time. About once a week, I would tell the scouts I had an appointment. What they didn't know was that I was seeing a counselor. Specifically, a Military and Family Life Counselor. The benefit of going to one of them is that they don't write anything down unless you say you want to harm someone or yourself.

I used this to keep my emotions under control for a while. I would vent about how much I didn't like being a scout. I never told them about any of the blackmail or scams that happened to me. In fact, before I wrote this book, no one ever knew. I don't even recall telling them about incidents involving my father or mother. Maybe I felt even a counselor couldn't save me.

One day, I worked up the courage to tell that counselor how I really felt. Over the past couple of months, I was thinking about how I could end my life. In that moment, I could feel my voice in my throat, almost like I was being choked. Tears were building up in my eyes, but I don't recall if they ever fell. I believe, in that moment, I found my voice, which I had silenced many years ago.

It took me months to find thirty seconds of courage, a call for help.

What kept me from admitting that truth was the fear of retaliation. The combat mindset states that you are weak if you ask for help. But what I found out from this one act of courage was that it was all a lie I had told myself. There was not a single comment that discouraged me from admitting that I had a problem.

The problem wasn't them; it was me. I was in a platoon of about thirty people, and only one of them had any idea of what I was going through. Make sure that your team—whoever they are—knows you, and that you know them. Too many lives have been lost to the silence of the lies we tell ourselves.

By continuing to tell our stories—not just mine, but yours as well—we can take the impossible out of someone else's story.

THE EQUATION

We often use metaphors to paint a picture and teach a lesson. Here is the easiest way I can demonstrate the power of thinking outside the box.

We know that 1 + 1 = 2. This will always equal 2, but now you know how to make 2.

Let's ramp it up: 2 + 2 = 4. We took the two numbers we knew to double our result.

But if I wanted to make 5, I would need to find out how to make 3.

So, then we do 1 + 2 = 3.

We can now show that 3 + 2 = 5, but say we wanted to make 8. Because we know how to make 3 and 5, we already know how to make 8, too. Now here are some ways to make 9.

$$1 + 1 + 1 + 1 + 1 + 1 + 1 + 1 + 1 = 9$$

$$1 + 2 + 1 + 2 + 1 + 2 = 9$$

$$3 + 3 + 3 = 9$$

$$5 + 4 = 9$$

What you need to see is that changing your mind works very similarly. Once you figure out one question, you can then use that answer to help with the next question. The more you know, the more efficient you become. *You already know the answer; you just need to plug in the correct numbers.*

IT ONLY TAKES ONE QUESTION

In 2019, when I started to reconstruct my mind, there was no book, no quote, no guide, and no clear answer—just a single question that would go on to change my life.

That life-changing question is different for each of us. For some of you, it is "What if...?" For others, it is "How am I going to do this?" For me, it was "Do I want to die?" Asking myself that one question planted a seed in my brain.

That seed would then grow into a tree with many branches, leaves, and flowers. When you ask yourself one hard question, it will typically lead to a series of questions. That is how this book came to be written.

When a tree first sprouts, it starts small and can be easily stepped on. Once the seed has been planted, you then need to supply it with sun and water. It takes years of dedication to turn a seed into a tree. The strongest trees have the most rings. If you cut a tree down, you will see a layer for each year that the tree has been around. Those layers are the questions you ask yourself, while the trunk, as a whole, represents your overall mindset. The roots represent your core values in life, which absorb nutrients and nourish your mindset.

Those hard questions you ask yourself will determine how strong your mindset will become. The water and sun make up the actions required to grow that mindset. The branches mirror the paths you choose to take in life. A new branch is flimsy and can break at any time, but it can also grow many leaves and flowers, the fruits of your labor—perhaps a life you changed, a goal achieved, a fortune you made, or a new skill learned.

But some trees will never grow leaves or flowers. Some will have empty branches. Perhaps the wrong environment blocked out the sunlight. Maybe you planted a bad seed. Sometimes even the most flourishing trees get struck by lightning. But a tree always starts by planting a seed. What it will grow into depends on you.

COMPLETE HONESTY

To truly change your mind requires complete honesty. Perhaps you avoid honesty because you're afraid of the answers you will find in yourself. But embracing honesty is the only way to get yourself out of your current situation. If you want to change but you're not honest with yourself, then you are bound to repeat the same mistakes. *Lies offer you a temporary solution but lead you down a road of misery.*

Nothing good ever comes from a lie, even if that lie has some partial truth in it. *Lying to someone seeking the truth will only lead them down a path of misadventure.*

My own lie always hid in plain sight, disguised by an emotionless exterior. The lie I always told people was: "I'm doing fine."

People always took my word; no one ever inquired further. Maybe if society asked beyond *how* a person is doing to uncover *why* they feel that way, we would all find more transparency. Saying "I'm doing fine" is easy. But if anyone had asked me why, I would not have had an answer. Perhaps it might have saved me a trip to the hospital if they had dug a little further. (Isolation is, of course, what inevitably landed me there.)

These are some of the thoughts I often have now, looking back on my life. The more I find out about myself, the faster I can help others find their light. *It's a search that I will never find an end to but will always pursue.* Eventually, there will be no more lessons for me to learn in the dark. When that happens, I must find a new way to acquire knowledge.

Reader, I hope you find these lessons valuable as you continue. But for now, I will leave you with this insight: *In truth, you will find redemption.*

Reflective Question:
- What is the truth you are hiding from?

WHY I CHOSE TO LIVE

During the time I contemplated suicide, I asked myself one question: *Do I want to die?* The answer to that was no—the same for many people who reach this point in life. When I was in the hospital, I discovered an important fact: Most people who are suicidal don't want to end their lives. They want people to recognize the struggles they are going through. When they don't see a way forward, that's when they take their life.

That is the fundamental reason why writing this book is essential to me. Someone out there needs to know they're not alone. My hope is that by the end of the story, everyone can see that.

That person I was back in 2019 was a former shadow of myself. I was broken; I made decisions that made me sick to my stomach. But I realized there was a better way, that I could be better, that *what happened to me did not have to define me.*

I realized that *I did not want to die before I had lived.* Most people go through the motions, making it through life out of habit. When you hold the world in the palm of your hand, that privilege often keeps you from living life to your fullest potential. Instead, you settle for an average life, never pursuing your true purpose.

VULNERABILITY

I asked you the most challenging question I had: "What is the hard question that you are avoiding asking yourself?" It is only fair for me to ask myself the same question. There are two answers I could give you, but I know which one I must choose.

The first question is, *Have I changed?* The answer is yes; otherwise, I would not have written this book.

Now, the second one brings me back to the most vulnerable time in my life, and to the most controversial part of this book. That question I often avoid asking myself is, *What if that age scam wasn't a scam at all?* What if that night was real?

Does the answer change the story or how you view me? Did a stranger really give me a second chance at life?

I often think about that night. I believe this is where the book gets its power: the vulnerability of showing you my lowest point in life, a truth that has "canceled" many others. I believe this question is something I must be open about. Otherwise, my dishonesty with myself and with you would ruin any future chance of success I have.

You cannot run from your fears and regrets in life. Once you try to run from a lion, its instincts kick in. The chase is now on, and your options are minimal. If the lion catches you, it's over. The other approach is to face the lion head-on. Sure, it will still try to attack, but you avoid the dread of the chase. You have taken the fun out of the game. The lion knows that you are no longer easy prey.

By being vulnerable and revealing my past, I hope to show you that my mistake is not who I am. A true predator would hide his intentions rather than be open, admit fault, and take responsibility. A predator also wouldn't feel shame for what he did. He would try to justify his actions, which I have not done and will not do. I talk about it not to glorify it, but to raise awareness of what happens when you let darkness consume you.

By doing so, maybe I can stop someone from making the same mistakes I made. If the message is too late, then at least I can show you that it's possible to find your redemption, as well. That is all I can hope for in this situation. But in the end, nothing ever goes away; eventually, someone will find those messages, and the answer will be found. When that happens, I suppose it will be up to you to make that judgment of my character, to hate or forgive, to prosecute or understand.

WHY I WROTE THIS BOOK

I have been wondering why I wrote this book for the last couple of months. Looking back at my life, I see that I have gone through significant hardships, ones that would make many people give up on life. But here I am, still standing and making progress when all the odds have been against me.

As I said before, I grew up poor. I did not have many friends as a kid, and I isolated myself from the world. I didn't have my first relationship until I had reached adulthood. I failed both in school and in the military. While everyone else was living it up, each new day brought me closer to death.

I had numerous opportunities to lean on generational trauma, and perhaps I was entitled to do so, like so many others before me. But I *chose* not to, despite everything that happened to me. I eventually sought out answers on my own. *I went deep inside my brain and figured out how to turn depression into happiness, trauma into lessons, and addictions into abstinence.*

Reflective Question:
- If you were to write a book about your life, how would that book help others?

CHAPTER 3

RESTORING FAITH

We must first restore what you have forgotten before we can start over.

GOING TO WAR WITH GOD

The title may sound extreme, but my coming to terms with faith took decades. Even recently, when I found it, it was only weeks ago that I broke a nine-year streak of not going to church. The last time I went to church before that was after my mother's death. But my war with God started long before then.

My mother was the leading advocate for going to church. So, when she left this world too soon, I didn't have anyone forcing me to go. Even when I found faith, I still didn't go to church. Perhaps there is still some resistance in me after all these years. Still some unresolved issues that even I don't know about.

But I suppose a mother knows what's best for her children even before they do. In my teenage years, I was not church material to say the least. I was a silent, hard-rock kid with a hardened heart. Hardened to a world that helped create a character that I still hate to this day—the character who saw no good left in the world and no future with me in it.

I was dressed head to toe in clothing that would defy Christ himself. Many different hair styles: some days it was blue, other times I wore it with liberty spikes—perhaps a warning not to get too close. The music I listened to also was not shy about actively rebelling against Heaven. Among my favorite artists is the *Antichrist Superstar* himself, Marilyn Manson.

My favorite shirt would reference that with the phrase "Born American, Antichrist by choice," showing an American flag adorned with the Antichrist symbol. It was my dad's old shirt from the nineties that he gave to me as I got into heavier music. A shirt older than me, decaying away just like my faith in God.

I even had a sweater of Manson's that I would wear year-round, even when it was ninety degrees outside. I was not shy about being in church with it, either; I defied their beliefs. But they never tried to stop me, even though my mom would specifically ask me not to wear it during church. She knew what he stood for; she would still take me to his concert when he came to Illinois.

During one song, he would have a Bible on the podium and begin tearing it up. Once the pages were torn, he would throw them into the audience. I felt bad for that part, so I told my mom she may want to close her eyes.

Despite all of this, she still wouldn't harass me to get rid of the materials or my beliefs. She knew something that I didn't yet. If you even mentioned church, Bibles, or Christ Himself, you lost me immediately, and I would tune you out—it took me over ten years to figure out what I'm about to share with you in this passage.

Although my mother and I didn't get along, I still remember

one particular phrase she said to me. She told me that one day I would return, that God had already promised it to her. The bravery it took for her to speak that cannot be put into words. To be able to openly say the word of God to someone who hated him with all his heart. To actively allow her son to turn to darkness, keeping faith he would turn back.

It was a promise she would not see fulfilled during her time in this world. God sometimes has a weird way of testing true faith. To give something only once you are gone. She suffered terribly in life, but somehow she always kept her faith in God. But we all have a reason for being; some purposes in life can only be seen in retrospect.

After her death, I was given her journal—small and purple, her favorite color. I kept that journal for about six years before I actually took the time to read it, mainly because I was still resistant to faith, which I knew was its primary purpose. I don't plan to discuss the journal's contents, but I will tell you one thing I put together while reading it.

She didn't say it in words, but I could tell she knew her time in this world was coming to an end. As I realized this, tears welled in my eyes. She had known the entire time but didn't want to tell anyone. I guess that is why she called me one last time, before my birthday, to say a final goodbye without my knowing.

Here she was suffering her entire life, praising God, while I, on the other hand, had a finger toward the sky. I was given a second chance, while she was not. Some may argue that this was a cruel act, but no, it is proof that there is a God—a loss of one life in exchange for another to be saved in the future.

The words *faith* and *belief* are referenced throughout this book by the same person over a hundred times, someone who wanted nothing to do with God his entire life. By the end of the book, you surely must realize there is a God, writing the stories behind the scenes. There is one story within the Bible that explains it all, though I assume most people fear it or skim by it.

It is now my favorite biblical story, bringing this entire book and its concepts together into a cohesive whole. You will see it scattered throughout the book, and it gives context to many unsolved questions in the world. For me, it's the story of Job's life.

The book of Job tells a tale of a wealthy man who worshipped God. A man whom *even God* spoke highly of. But one day, the Devil walks up to God and makes a bet that he can change Job's faith. The bet, of course, is that Job will lose his faith once the Devil is allowed to bring misfortune upon him. So then, one by one, the Devil takes everything Job has been given—his wealth, his children, and his health. Even his close friends say that God himself must have cursed Job. Though he doesn't understand, Job remains faithful throughout the story.

Many people would say this is unjust or unnecessary suffering, but that is where we get it wrong. It is in this one book that many of the world's secrets lie, and the one that made my story make sense to me. It wasn't until I found faith that I was able to discover the same secret: that it was not just a story about Job, but about every person in the world.

It was never a bet with the Devil, but a choice. It is a ritual that every man and woman will face in their life. God loves us so much that he knows we must first be offered to the darkness before we are brought to the light. Not a bet, but the ultimate choice of free will. Not from a place of fear, but by willingly submitting yourself to a greater purpose despite what pain comes your way.

The greater the suffering you are faced with in life, the more you know you are marked by both God and the Devil. Instead of coming from wealth, it was given to me when I had nothing but suffering. My war with God started as a young child, and it took until adulthood to realize I was fighting the wrong side.

The Devil had to place his bet early, in fear of what was to come. Sometimes, we must first walk in hell to find the light within ourselves. I couldn't find my answers in the Bible; I was too resistant. I first had to see God in my story. God had to offer me to the Devil to help me find true faith.

The instability, the suffering, the loneliness—all were chapters to be added to this book. But be careful when going to war with God. He will always give you what you believe in. I hated people, so he gave me a reason to hate them. I hated the Army, so he gave me a reason to hate it even more. I hated myself, and he gave me reasons to hate myself.

It was in the moment of my choosing life when my war with God finally ended.

FINDING FAITH

I still struggle with faith. It's not that I don't have faith; I am just still asking myself those hard questions about it. Maybe I was on the wrong side. Negativity and hatred often do not mix well with faith.

Faith requires belief in something before reaching a determined outcome. But growing up, I looked at the world from what I believed was a realistic standpoint. Faith leads to many questions without answers. Now, instead of looking at the lack of answers, I try to theorize and develop my views on how I would answer them.

You can find the mark of this philosophy throughout this book, not just this section. As I investigated faith, I began to see a correlation: The more faith you have, the more positive your outlook. Perhaps this is because faith focuses on the outside of ourselves. When we're not navel-gazing, we can see something more to be revealed in life.

Suffering, pain, death, sadness, anger—there is a purpose in even the worst experiences in life. Speaking for myself, those experiences led to many answers in this book; without faith, I'm not sure any of it would be possible. *For faith to work, you must forget about sight and instead unlock your mind.*

WHEN YOU HAVE NOTHING

When it feels like the world has turned its back on you.

When you think there is nothing good left in it.

When you try your best to make a change, only to repeatedly fail over and over again.

When you have nothing left, that is when you must believe in something, though belief will differ from person to person.

Some of you will look toward a high power. Perhaps you feel that you have dug yourself so deep into a hole that it would take a miracle to save you. For others, once you take a look in the mirror, you will remember who you were supposed to believe in. Whatever it is, man or God, you must believe in something.

If you believe in nothing, then that is what you shall receive until you make a choice. As it has been said throughout time, the person who thinks they can and the person who thinks they can't are both typically right. If you don't believe in yourself, then why should anyone else? Maybe you'll be the lucky person who has someone to believe in you before you do, but *the only one who can change your mind is you.*

WHY DO YOU NEED TO BELIEVE IN SOMETHING?

You need to believe in something because, when you believe in nothing, you will always be wrong. There are two paths you could go down when you believe in nothing. For these examples, we will use religion as a base.

If you believe in nothing, let's say you are right—let's say there is no God, no afterlife, and everything we do has been for nothing. When you die, you become nothing: no soul, no voice, no one to comfort you, just a void of nothingness. To me, being sentenced to nothingness is a fate far worse than death or Hell itself.

Now let's say that you were wrong—that there is God, an afterlife, and, by implication, a Hell. You have lived how you wanted to, ignoring some of the fundamental laws of God and telling yourself they do not exist. In this case, I hope, for your sake, that you were a decent human being, and that God feels merciful on the day of your judgment.

I'm not asking you to follow my views on what I worship or even to share my beliefs. But I want you to consider at least this: If you believe in nothing, it doesn't matter whether you are right or wrong. Neither path will have the outcome you want. If you at least believe in some version of God and are the best person you can be, it is better than not believing at all. Even if it is the wrong god, it is better to admit you're wrong than deny any existence at all.

Perhaps you're a person who needs to see the facts. Many could argue that all Bibles are made by man and not God, which leads to interpretation rather than straight facts. But if it were all facts and you could see God every day, it wouldn't be as special. It would take away the most important aspect of religion, which is faith.

Believing in something before you have the proof is true faith.

WHAT IS STRONGER—FAITH OR HOPE?

Here's my definition of faith: belief before reaching a determined outcome.

On the other hand, here's my definition of hope: a wish for a better outcome.

Jordan Peterson describes belief as something you would die for. To reach that point, you need a strong justification.

A wish doesn't require anything except desire. For this reason, faith will always be stronger than hope to me.

Here are two examples to demonstrate the difference between the two:

One says, "I have *faith* I will pass the test."

The other says, "I hope I will pass the test."

Without any context, the faith sentence sounds much stronger. But why is that?

I believe the answer is that when you have faith in something, it implies that you trust the work you have done before the present moment. By saying, "I hope I will pass," you imply that you are relying on luck or wishing without doing the work. *When you hope for something, you do nothing and expect it to happen.* When you have faith, you hold a belief and conduct actions that justify that belief. Always remember: *Faith acts; hope does not.*

DO YOU BELIEVE IN FREE WILL?

Two of the big mysteries of the world are whether God exists and what humanity's role is in this world. Skeptics often ask, "If God is so great, then why is there so much evil in the world?"

My answer: *It is not God who is evil, but the deeds caused by the free will of men and women.*

I genuinely do believe we have free will, which is why life fascinates me. We can choose to change the world through peaceful speech or kill it with violence. If everyone did good deeds, then there would be no point in life or the afterlife. While on Earth, we have a purpose, but whether we find it is on us.

God allows our free will because he is not looking for perfection. He is looking for someone who chooses to walk in faith. Despite the world's harsh treatment of the fallen, they have every right to be the villain and choose to be the hero. Think of it this way: When choosing a leader, would you want someone who inherited the role as a birthright or someone who earned the role with their right actions?

WHAT IF EVERYONE WAS PERFECT?

The world isn't supposed to be perfect—that's a core belief of mine. We are here to have our worth tested. Are you worthy of taking the next step in life? Life isn't about suffering; it's about how much suffering we can endure and keep going.

If everyone were perfect, there would be no point in creating this world. Perfectly good or evil are the domains of Heaven and Hell, not Earth. Imperfect people prove that there is free will in this world just by existing. If it were all destined, there would be no final lesson, no meaning for the pain.

If we were all perfect, everyone would be God—and if everyone were God, then none of us would be.

Reflective Question:
- Do you believe in perfection?

MY BIGGEST STRUGGLES WITH FAITH

I have struggled with faith my entire life. Even as a child, I didn't always have faith—not because the world was harsh to me, but because I didn't know how to believe in something I couldn't see. I had to grow up quickly to make it in this world.

Pessimism and faith are opposites, making faith difficult for pessimists to understand. When pessimism no longer served me, faith began to take root. I needed faith to give me a reason behind all the pain I had endured. I knew I could no longer do life on my own, and eventually I conceded that I needed a higher power to guide me.

My first reconnection with faith was through tarot readings. Tarot helped me feel connected to something beyond myself—something that seemed to speak directly to what I was going through. That gave me my faith back when I needed it most. It provided me with a way to talk to God, spirits, or angels—whichever you prefer. Maybe my connection to tarot was a bit biased, since I've always loved card games, but that makes this method more personal for me.

Another issue I have with faith is that religious texts are all written by men. Sacred texts leave faith up to the interpretation of the author. I think this is where we lose a lot of people, in trying to describe a perfect being as an imperfect creation. I believe it is essential to decipher what resonates with you as you read those texts.

I'm still forming the right question to gain the answer I am searching for in life. But I think that search is part of life, in the end. We are supposed to ask these questions—not to provoke God, but to help us understand Him. The same can be seen when a shepherd rejoices over finding a lost sheep—one out of one hundred.

God rejoices over the people who have struggled with faith their entire lives, who questioned it at every opportunity, but eventually chose to believe. This is most satisfying—to gain favor not by force, but by their free will.

Faith didn't find me in a moment of peace. It came after long years of questioning, doubts, and finally, a need to believe in something more.

Reflective Question:
- Do you avoid belief out of doubt, out of fear of being wrong, or something else?

CHAPTER 4

THE POWER OF THE MIND

The mind is what lost faith, so now we must rebuild our thoughts.

A GLIMPSE INTO HELL

When you find yourself on the road to Hell, you realize in that moment Heaven is also real.

I allowed you a small glimpse of what happened in 2019, but now I'm going to give you the whole story.

Without this part of my life, I'm not so sure this book would ever have been written. Funny how that works. The worst days of our lives are what will give others hope in finding their own redemption. I bash on the word hope in the previous chapter, but hope is where one must start when you have nothing. Eventually, once you put in the work, hope turns into faith.

When I had no faith left, hope was my only chance to make it through this experience.

I'll be honest, I can't give you an exact timeline of the events I'm about to share. Most of them have been erased from my life because it all happened so long ago. Maybe it's best that way, to not have all the information, making it easier to move on with life's worst decisions. I'm not even sure where or how to start this section.

But we must start somewhere, and I imagine it began sometime during the ninety-day detail at Fort Knox. That's where my hatred for the Army spawned, but when I traveled back to Fort Hood, I began to hate myself. My heart started to take a backseat while my brain slowly fell into depression.

I would look at the rest of the platoon partying on the weekends, telling their wild stories while I silently sat alone in the barracks. It was in that isolation that I developed the character that I hate—filling my head with a false narrative of being the biggest loser in the world.

Here I was, twenty-one years old, never having been on a date. I had been rejected my entire life, both in popularity and by those I had asked out in the past. I had nothing going for me in this life, no desirable features, no stories of my own to tell—just an empty shell with no will to live. I just wanted what everyone else had at the time: a life and someone to share it with.

So, I followed what everyone else did: I tried online dating, which is where my life got worse. At first, I tried Tinder, which was the popular app at the time. I started slowly but eventually became addicted. Not the kind of addiction you are thinking about, though. No, I didn't get hooked on dates; instead, I found an addiction of desperation.

Looking back, those dating websites are quite predatory in how they operate, especially to those who are not top-tier males in the genetic pool. There is a regular app in which you swipe left or right depending on whether you like each person's profile. After a couple of swipes, the site will turn it off for the day. They offer you a premium version to keep going.

Then there is the golden package for the few as desperate as I was. This package allows you to be seen by more women. It gives you unlimited swiping, the ability to super-like profiles, and more control over what you choose to view. Most of the other Soldiers would poke fun at people who had paid for these apps, which is why I always kept quiet.

What's even worse is that to keep you on the website, I assume they have bots to like your profile. I can only imagine, given that half of them have nearly blank profiles and never respond or message. But I was already hooked. I grew up poor, so once I got hold of money, I had a hard time keeping it.

Day by day, month by month, I fell into a vicious cycle of spending money on dating websites. The fundamental part that got me hooked was that I never found anyone. The entire city within a one-hour radius had rejected me. The only people left for me were the bots, catfishers, and most importantly, the scammers.

I must have spent thousands of dollars on all the accounts by the end. I went to every site possible. When I ran out of the radius on one app, I just went to the next with the same desperation. When I say every app, I really mean every app I could find—even those apps with one-star reviews, warning about bots and scammers.

It got to the extent that I went past the app store. When the app store failed, I even tried looking at adult websites. Yeah, those ads that pop up, which probably give your laptop a virus as you click on them. Those go past the boundaries of even the normal dating websites and are somehow even more predatory.

I learned to read the fine print after using those websites. It didn't take too long before they spread my debit card information to their other websites. The lowest form of desperation can be found on those websites. If you think the Tinder bots are bad, these will hit you with twenty messages the moment you make a profile.

That's how they reel you in; they make it seem like you're the best person to have visited their website. But it never leads anywhere except an empty wallet. The worst part is that once you're in, it's extraordinarily hard to get your information out of the system. I have tried for a very long time to erase my old profiles.

It's to the extent that even in 2025, I still get random emails from people across different platforms. My information and exploitive photos are still lost somewhere out there in the world. Once it's on the internet, it will always be there. Perhaps one day I will eventually escape that world for good, but I know it's only a matter of time before someone starts searching for what I tried to bury.

A couple of pages in, and I haven't even begun to tell the stories of the people I actually met. You would think that having my information out on the web was the worst part. But we have merely scratched the surface—just a small glimpse of the hell I got myself into.

The best way I can describe this next part of the story is the compound effect—a chain of events that starts small and gets worse each time. One percent repeated each day, normally, is how you can start a good habit. But what happens when the 1 percent goes in the wrong direction? How deep must one dig a hole before one realizes it's their own grave?

In the beginning, it started small. Probably the most memorable experience I had was with a woman we will call "D" to protect any real names. I assume it was a catfishing situation, and it was the longest interaction I've had. In fact, every once in a while, D will still reach out to me with different numbers, begging for another chance at the wallet.

She is the one I had gotten most comfortable with, and comfort in this case was not good. She was never sexual and never blackmailed me in any way. Instead, we had regular conversations and sent each other photos throughout the day. This kept me caught in the web for a long time. The first time she asked for money, I was already hesitant.

Hesitant to the fact that I had been rejected by hundreds, if not thousands, of people by this time. When looking at her photos, she was always out of my league. Nothing extreme to throw the radar off completely, which is why she was able to get away with it for a while, I guess.

But it was the same old story: Send her money to visit. But she always found an excuse never to show up. One time, it was the hospital; another time, she got scared or just completely missed the trip. She would also never accept a ticket; it was only cash, which was the biggest giveaway. This interaction had been going on for months.

Although I knew it was a scam by this point, I went as far as I possibly could to prove it. I concluded that if she wouldn't come to me, I would go to her. One of the dumber moves on my end: I took a bus down to the city she was staying in and got a hotel room. Gave her the address, which was only a couple of blocks down the road.

But somehow she kept making excuses for why she couldn't come down. She even made a story about being stuck at the hospital. Desperate as I was, I eventually just walked down to that hospital in the middle of the night, to once again find no evidence of this being a real person. D's most extreme request was trying to get me to marry her before even meeting her in person.

I can't tell you how dumb this decision was—walking to that hospital that night. In hindsight, the city was sketchy on its own.

Homeless people were living under a bridge, and all the stores had been closed, with some wood blocking off broken windows or doors. If anyone wanted to harm me, I could have disappeared and never been found. But this was just the beginning and one of the tamer experiences. I probably gave D a couple of thousand dollars alone.

From here, it only got worse. Instead of the catfishing, I started running into more vicious people. The next was one I believe I found on an adult website. Conversations were quicker, and I don't think I need to go into full detail for you to know where it went next. At first, they were nice, but eventually they led down the same road as D.

I would send them money to help with their current situations. Their stories were a little different, and maybe that's why I was more gullible. Their cover was that they fell into a predatory contract, they were promised a good life, and they themselves were exploited. Essentially, they were being forced to post on these sites against their will.

I would give them what they asked for to be the hero of the story. But just like D, they never showed up. It never ended, either, but eventually I stopped sending them funds. When that happened, it was the first time I experienced blackmail. I was told to send them money, or they would release our conversations and photos online. They eventually left me alone for a while, which let me get enough breath to find myself in my next scam.

The next one cut straight to the chase and was again from another sketchy website. I knew something was up from the first sentence and the request, but I gave it to them anyway. We were sending photos back and forth, which led to their asking for a photo with my face in an exploitive position.

Within thirty seconds of my sending that photo, they sent

me a screenshot of my family's Facebook profile pictures. Out of all the scams I ran into, these people were the most vicious; the others hadn't involved personal matters. These went straight for the jugular. What choice did I have but to give them what they wanted?

Later, when the first blackmailing scammer came back, she actually helped me. She told me how the industry worked. They had no intention of sending the photo, but they wanted to see how much they could get out of me. They were looking for a helpless victim who wouldn't fight back.

When that happened, it was recommended that I block the number and delete the profile, which I did. For all my family who decided to continue reading on, now you know why I disappeared from Facebook for a long time. Once I returned to Facebook, I kept my profile private for years. I've only made it public again upon writing this book.

But we know this still isn't the end of this story. Despite all of this, I continued. There is one more story, before we get to the big one, that I was very hesitant to write about. I don't want anything off the table at this point. I want you to know everything—not to exploit myself, but to show you that Hell is real and you can't possibly deny it.

This next one was real. No catfisher, no scammer, no bot. It was the first real person I had encountered in over a year of searching. The catch? Well, she wanted money, of course, and I was willing to give it to her. I couldn't stand the feeling of being alone anymore. She was the only honest person I met during this time; at least she didn't hide what she was doing.

What I gave up that night was something I can never get back.

I had no vehicle at the time, so I grabbed an Uber around midnight. I went to the gas station to get the money she had asked me to withdraw. Next, I arrived at her place. It was on the poor side of the neighborhood. The door was locked, and it had a metal casing. She unlocked it, looked around briefly, and then let me in. I was escorted to an empty room.

In that room was a mattress tucked away in a corner. Next to it were some tissues and a condom. She turned the light off, sat on the mattress, and then had me strip down until there was nothing left. She set an alarm for one hour.

I visited her one more time after that. It was a short visit at a different location. Out of curiosity, I asked her why she did it, and she said it was to get some extra money. I will go into the details of why I stopped going shortly, but I first want to pause for a moment.

I know that everything I did throughout this time was bad—there's nothing about this part of my life I'm proud of. But what scares me—and one of the many reasons I'm writing this story into the book specifically—is that it's getting worse out there. We are reaching a point in society where events like these are becoming normal on the internet.

Sites like OnlyFans are promoting this kind of behavior, taking in people in exchange for photos, videos, and even sexual acts regularly. Bonnie Blue is best known for sleeping with a thousand men in a single day. Women turning eighteen, like Lil Tay, starting on OnlyFans the day of their birthday and selling explicit videos, are making over $1 million in some cases.

It makes me question how far we are going to take it as a society before we have to say no. People like me were a part of the problem, but the road goes both ways, unfortunately. How many more people need to be used and exploited before we draw the line?

But my rant is over—back to the story you came to hear.

After the second visit, I went to work the next morning, but something was very off that day. When I woke to go to the bathroom as usual, I found myself in there again within a minute. It was one of those situations where you go to pee, but even when you're done, it feels like you have to go again.

Once I got to work, it didn't stop, and it was getting worse. After the third time, my section leader made a joke about hanging out with sketchy women and getting the clap. Little did he know that for me it wasn't a joke. I went to the bathroom for about the tenth time within an hour. Every five minutes, I had to go back; a burning sensation kept dropping me to my knees. If you have ever seen *The Green Mile*, you would get a visual image of the pain I went through.

It was on that last trip that I discovered something terribly wrong was going on. I started to pee blood into the urinal, and it also began to turn into mucus. Instead of a stream, it turned blood-red and thick. It was at that point that I figured my section leader might have been right. Without him ever knowing, I found out that he was.

I went to the clinic after that to get tested; it's a very awkward check-up. They also suspected I had some kind of STD. I had to strip down to give them a sample. Eventually, it came back, and I tested positive for Chlamydia. Luckily, it is curable, and I was back to normal soon. That was the last time I ever did something sketchy like that, but unfortunately, my troubles were not over yet.

The last big story was one I already told you a little bit about—the age scam. The one that eventually sent me to the hospital. But I never went into full detail about what actually happened. Like I said in the first chapter, it was a typical profile until we started talking.

The first thing that happened was they swapped the age and sent an exploitive photo. I got that gut-wrenching feeling in my stomach as if I was going to vomit. Even though every part of me told me this was the time to back away, I continued to give them exactly what they sent me.

The next day, as you know, I was confronted over the phone by a man claiming to be the girl's father. I can still remember the exact location where I received that call, and the first words out of his mouth were: "Young man, you're in big trouble." I was at work on my way back to lunch at the barracks. But at that moment, I froze in place. I knew exactly where this conversation was going, so I asked if I could call him back once I was in the room.

Most people would not have called back, and perhaps that is what saved me if it were a real experience. He explained that his daughter was in the hospital because, after he and his wife saw our conversation, his daughter had tried to commit suicide. I then had two options: help pay the bills, or they would turn me in.

It was shortly after that when I also put myself in the hospital. Even after I got out, they were still asking me for money. It was when I told them that I had no money and I was also ready to end my life that they finally left me alone. It wasn't until the end of the scenario that I realized this may have been another scam.

I cannot imagine how much money I spent over this time frame. I still have some receipts totaling over $3,000 for only two months. But this experience lasted for over a year. I still have one of the receipts from this age dilemma. Maybe one day I'll work up the courage to confront them.

It wasn't until a year or two later that I fully believed it was a scam. But that, my friend, is a story and a test for another day.

YOU CAN MAKE YOURSELF DEPRESSED

This is one of the lessons I learned on my trip to the hospital. Did you know that you can be in a perfectly normal state of mind, but if you convince yourself you are depressed, then your mind will follow that belief? I don't want to diminish the self-hatred I experienced at that time. That part was genuine and will always be a fact. You can't change your past, but you can control what you do now, in the present.

I want you to understand the power of our beliefs and minds. Once I learned how the mind works, my life started to change. Eventually, I asked myself, *If I believed I was depressed and made myself depressed, what would happen if I thought that I was happy?* That is the premise of this entire book and the reason I am alive today.

> Reflective Question:
> - What is your current mindset, and does it need to change?

WHAT DO YOU SAY TO YOURSELF?

No one has said anything worse to me than what I have said to myself. The hardest person in my life to please has almost always been me. I constantly remind myself and others, "If you would never say that to someone else, why would you say it to yourself?" Negative thinking erodes self-esteem. At first, you're being hard on yourself, and the next moment, you hate who you are.

But sometimes "tough love" has a place and a purpose. Back in 2019, I used to view myself as a loser, and there was some truth behind that. I wasted my time in the digital world and avoided living my actual life. I gave my money to people who had only bad intentions toward me.

I want to examine the negative thoughts that preceded this time in my life. They're why it's essential to choose wisely what you say to yourself. If you don't, then what's going to stop that self-fulfilling prophecy from coming true?

I am not perfect and never will be. I have issues just like everyone else. That part of me still resides deep within—I think we all have it—the person who wants nothing but the world's downfall. For me, *he's like an old friend that I have outgrown. He never stays too long; he knows he is no longer welcome in my house.*

Reflective Question:
- Are you being hard on yourself or overly critical?

DO I REGRET SOME OF THE DECISIONS I MADE AT THAT TIME?

I believe regret is an ordinary and necessary part of life. Would I take back my actions if I could? That is an entirely different question, and the answer would be no.

It was during my darkest moments that I first began to look for the light.

Neither my father's outburst nor my mother's death put me in the hospital. My lack of accountability in my own life did. When I left for the military, that was my time to make a change. Even that change was only partially successful. But that still didn't give me the right to be consumed with darkness.

Without those bad decisions, I would not be here today, nor could I share with you how I got through those hard times. *Those tough times—the ones we wish never happened—are often what help us start fresh.*

THINK INDEPENDENTLY

Thinking independently does not mean you have to do everything in isolation. Now, if you are in the dark part of your life, you may have no other choice except to go it on your own. Either way, you must go into your mind and make your own decisions. No one can do that for you. *They can help you along the way if you get lost, but it is your path to walk.*

I also encourage you to challenge yourself to do it without overreliance on medication. Sometimes, medication is necessary. But you can overcome many emotional states by exploring your mind and learning to control them. Then again, I'm not a medical provider; I am just a person telling his story. This decision, like everything else, is ultimately yours.

When I was in the hospital in 2019, a psychiatric provider gave me a prescription to help with my negative thinking. I tried it for a little while, but I concluded I didn't need it and set out to find the answers on my own. Today, I still hold onto that bottle to remind myself that I overcame my negative thought patterns on my own, not with medication, but by facing my emotions head-on.

It's important to note that I saw the negatives more than the average person. I had a bias against prescription medication due to my mother's death. It was harder to struggle on without meds. But I also skipped the withdrawal step that comes when someone develops a reliance on their medication.

DO YOU ALWAYS NEED TO APPLY ALL THE LESSONS?

Learn how to apply each of my lessons only when it is necessary and pertinent to you.

Let's take my own beliefs, as expressed in my philosophies and statements, as an example. Would I die for them, as Jordan Peterson claims? No, not all of them. However, some of my rules do have life-or-death importance to me. After all, some of them have saved my life.

The three philosophies I recounted at the beginning of the book are the rules I would die for:

1. Everything happens for a reason.
2. Accept what has happened.
3. Move on.

But not every rule in this book is universal or absolute.

For example, "Think independently" is meant to empower you to go inside your head and find the answers you seek. It is not meant to tell you to do everything alone. You shouldn't go to war alone, you shouldn't start an international business alone, and you can't be in a relationship alone. If you try, then you are bound to fail.

CHAPTER 5

FINDING YOUR PURPOSE

Now that you have regained your thoughts, it's time to choose a direction.

WHEN ALL IS LOST, SOMETHING IS FOUND

What do you do when you feel like you have reached the end of your story?

What do you do when the odds of making a comeback are slim to none?

At that moment, you only have one option: Something has to change. For me, change didn't happen overnight. It didn't happen in a day, a month, or even a year. For me to fully get my life back on track, it took between two and three years. I don't say this to scare you, but to prepare you.

When I began making my way out of Hell, I started with hope. Faith didn't happen until much later in my journey. I don't know if you can ever begin with faith, to believe in something before you have even started. But it is in that moment that something unexplainable happens. Despite everything that happened from my father's hospital trip all the way down to mine, there was a choice.

A choice to keep going. Perhaps that's the part of God that resides within us. When the voice within ourselves tells us this is the end, but another one says just one more day.

The day I got out of the hospital, *Answering the Hard Questions* spawned. But I had no idea at the time that nearly six years later it would turn into a book. But that's the part I love—not knowing where the world is going to take you day by day. The big picture can only be seen in retrospect.

I wonder what the old version of myself would think if he could see us now. I have even pondered what I would say to him back then. But it is only now that I know I would tell him nothing. To let me live the journey and figure it out for myself. If you are handed all the answers, then it wouldn't be a journey—now, would it? That is also why there are questions I won't answer for the reader; I don't want to steal the journey away from you.

Courage is what you will need most when starting over. Courage is not the absence of fear, but the act of facing it. No book can tell you what happens next. A motivational quote may provide some insight, but you will still have to find the answer within yourself. It started with me being able to sit down with myself once again.

But I know what you are thinking: How is it that I sat alone once again when I said that was where my issues spawned? There is a fundamental difference between being alone and being lonely. Being alone means walking with no one. Being lonely is just a feeling, which is why you can be alone but not lonely.

In that silent room, just me and a notebook, I began to discover myself once again. It was the ultimate battle between the mind and heart. The mind forms its ideas from what it sees and what has happened. But the heart already knows what you want before you do. The heart is just waiting for your mind to catch up.

When asking myself my first set of hard questions, I had to shut down my mind and let my heart speak. I had already chosen to live by putting myself in the hospital. But the next question I had to think about was how to move on with life. I was a pessimistic person at the time, so the first question was: *What would make me happy?*

I had to dig deep to answer that question. It had been at least five years of misery by this point in the story. It was the answer I had found in 2016—wanting to help people—but I lost it when I failed out of nursing school. I thought if I could help other people, maybe I could find the answers in my own life.

At the time, I was hoping they would separate me from the Army. It isn't out of the ordinary for that to happen if you have enough mental issues going on. I had to incorporate the Army into my answer. Back then, I still had years left on my contract. If I had told them what was actually going on in my life, no doubt they would have kicked me out. Six years later, I'm glad it never happened.

What they did was separate me from my old Scout Platoon. This actually helped me a lot in settling down the hatred I had developed. It also helped me see that it wasn't the Army I hated, but the job I was doing. They sent me to the training room, an office job where you help the company command team.

When I was in the Scout Platoon, the training room was almost used as a threat. It's where they would send the scouts who didn't belong or meet the standards they were looking for. But this job, I quite enjoyed. It was an independent job; you helped with Soldiers' paperwork, maintained the command vehicles, and tracked ongoing events.

Maybe it's because I felt unnoticed for so long. It was only when I left the Scout Platoon that I started making progress in my career. But there was also toxic leadership within the Scout Platoon. I knew this for a long time but chose not to speak about it until later. I never received any awards while in the Scout Platoon.

There was one incident in which I was supposed to receive an award, but they chose not to give it to me. We were doing a twelve-mile ruck march. The uniform consists of boots, OCP (Operational Camouflage Pattern) pants, a shirt, and an OCP top with at least thirty-five pounds worth of gear on your back, plus the weight of your water. It is also a timed event, fifteen minutes per mile or three hours total. It may sound slow, but go ahead and jump on a treadmill to try it yourself.

The ruck march is the most dreaded exercise event in the Army, and I include that on my list. It is extraordinarily rough and unhealthy for the body. Typically, by the end, pieces of skin will be falling off from blisters acquired halfway through. These blisters are accompanied by blood, usually dried up from your feet rubbing against your boots.

The bottoms of my feet were pale white from the excessive weight colliding with the hot cement throughout the event. The route wasn't very kind either; it was scheduled on Turkey Run—a road feared by most service members who know the running trails at Fort Hood. The reason for this is the hills' incline; the descent is nice until you realize you have to go back up.

In length, the hill is probably at least a quarter of a mile. When ascending, lean forward; otherwise, you may fall backward. There isn't just one hill, either; there is a series of them going up and down the entire time. It was a six-mile route, meaning once you were halfway and ready to drop your bag, you had to turn around to complete it again.

So, there I was, eight miles in, hating life; some people only had to do six miles, while I had to do twelve to go to Air Assault School. I was always a slow rucker, so I was by myself at this point. I caught up with another scout who was usually twenty to thirty minutes ahead of me on rucks. Turns out his water source had broken one mile in.

At eight miles, our OCP uniform, which is in different shades of green, had turned into a pool of sweat, and all the colors had nearly faded to black. By the end, we were pretty smoked. You drop your ruck, and you can see the steam come off your body, even though it's one hundred degrees outside. The problem for this other scout was that he ran out of sweat; there was no water left in him.

He said he was doing fine, so I went to pass him. I didn't have much time to lose, according to the halfway marker. Within thirty seconds, I could hear him collapse behind me. As a friend, I knew I couldn't just leave him there, so I circled back and then used my cell phone to call the vehicle to our location.

It must have taken them ten to fifteen minutes to reach us and get him the help he needed. This was time I could not afford to lose. I was ready to pack it in and get in that vehicle with him. But as David Goggins says, "When you think you're done, you're only 40 percent done." I didn't know any of his work back then, but he is right.

One of my old section leaders was there, and he knew I had more in me. It's in those small moments you see what you're truly capable of. I usually run and walk to keep a pace. But there was no time left to walk. I had to jog and sprint the rest of my time back. While I was past the central hills, the last quarter mile was a slow incline to add salt to the injury.

I had made it within the three-hour time limit and had ten minutes to spare. When I got down to drop the sack, they also had to weigh my bag to make sure I had the proper weight. Turns out I did have just thirty-five pounds with me, but over forty pounds of gear. It may sound small, but every pound counts when it comes to finishing these events out.

While I didn't think about it much, it was later revealed to me that the Scout Platoon OIC (Officer in Charge) was going to write me an award. By this time, I was walking past the office. But what he said after that shocked me. He said he didn't write the award because he got lazy and didn't feel like it. Why would he even tell somebody that? I would never have known about the award if he hadn't mentioned it, and he just threw it in my face.

I used this time in the training room to plan my escape. It was a temporary solution that gave me enough time to explore other military jobs. That led me to see my Career Counselor at the time, whom I had never heard of before. When I went in, he asked me to give him a list of jobs I was interested in.

One thing led to another, and eventually I asked him what his job was. I didn't yet know it, but that one question would change my life. I went home later that night to look further into the job description and what it entailed. I came back the next day, and I was hooked.

A Career Counselor is essentially someone who aligns the needs of the Army with the needs of the Soldier. We handle Soldiers' contracts to help them progress in their military careers or ensure they have a plan when preparing to leave. It's a selfless job, not consistently recognized, but very rewarding, knowing you can make a difference in someone's life every day.

This job lined up perfectly with the time I had left in the training room. There were a couple of requirements that I had to meet before I could get accepted. At the time, I was a Sergeant, but I needed a promotable status, which could take up to a year to receive. I also had to have six months at the company level to evaluate whether I could handle the job.

Our unit was preparing to deploy to Germany for nine months at the time. The command team had already told me that I would be in the training room for the duration. Everything was lined up just right to meet the requirements and complete the transition. My escape plan had been put into full motion.

This was the first long-term goal I'd made in my entire life. This goal would not only change my life but also save it. For the very first time, I knew what I was supposed to do. For years, I had been lost in a world that I didn't understand. It was when I set a goal and stuck to it that I found my purpose in life once again.

I found out that if you have set no goals, you will lack a sense of purpose in life. You are an archer without a target. How do you expect your aim to get better if you shoot at an open field? A student can never become a teacher if they are not willing to learn.

The goal is what I focused on to keep me on track and start this new life. It wasn't until six years down the road that I learned the most important thing about setting goals. It's not the end goal that's important, but who you become along the way.

WHAT IS MY ROLE?

Despite what you may think, I am not here to provide motivation; that comes with your part of the job. My goal is to guide you on your path to changing your mind.

Let's say it's the dead of winter. Your teeth are chattering, and you have no shelter. There's a single match left in the box, and you have already placed the branches you've collected for a fire in the pit.

I aim to light your fire. There is only one match because this may be your last chance to change your life for the better. The branches and pit represent your old views that no longer serve you in this new life. You have to destroy them to ensure your survival. The fire signifies your new mindset, one that continues to grow and provides warmth to get you through the winter.

Winter is your darkness. Its only goal is to extinguish your fire. *You must protect the flames; when the wind blows and the snow falls, you must build a shelter strong enough to withstand the harsh conditions of reality.* The shelter you create represents the physical and mental labor you must undertake. *You must have the courage to face your fears, the confidence to speak your beliefs, and the discipline to keep going.*

I know my role in your story. Do you know yours?

IS MOTIVATION NECESSARY?

This may be confusing for many people. You came here to get motivated and change your mind, but once again, you may be wrong. Now, while motivation is helpful, you don't need it to achieve your goal.

Think of the worst day of your life. At that time, you probably were not very motivated to do anything. When you're all alone and you don't know what to do, but you keep going anyway, it is proof that you don't always need motivation. When you were given a task that you didn't want to do, you probably were not motivated to do that, either.

Instead of motivation, I want you to find your purpose in life. What are you supposed to do in this world? *Yes, in that purpose, you will find motivation, but not everything in your purpose will give you motivation. The purpose shows you what is missing in your life, gives you a reason to keep going, and ignites the flame within you.*

AFTER I DECIDED TO LIVE

The first thing I did was start asking myself the hard questions. The first, and very challenging, question for me at the time was: *What will make me happy again?* I listed things that I liked to do before my depression set in, and I realized that I always felt called to help people.

As a scout, you have to be good at a couple of things. The first is that you need a good set of eyes. Mine are rather opposite; I have an eye so bad that they can't correct it. They won't even give me a Photorefractive Keratectomy (PRK) because it is too risky—there's the possibility it could damage my good eye and leave me with the bad one. I also recently found out I don't have depth perception, so what another scout sees or estimates doesn't physically make sense to me.

You also need to shoot well. In the scouting world, they use a lot of weaponry, including M4, M2 Browning, MK 19, M240, and the Bradley Fighting Vehicle. To give you an idea of my marksmanship, I have never qualified as an expert on any weapon system. I also got recycled in Basic Training for failing rifle marksmanship. Combine that with an inability to see my targets, and you've got a bad equation.

So, I had a couple of years left on my contract, and I investigated other jobs that I could do in the meantime. I chose to become a Career Counselor. I made it a goal to get this job, and anytime that I felt anger or frustration, I reminded myself of that goal until I achieved it.

Now, this was not always the most straightforward task. It took me about three years to even get to the school, and I also had setbacks that delayed the process. However, as I mentioned earlier, everything happens for a reason. I ended up finding a mentor who helped me secure a seat in a class.

Reflective Question:
- Maybe you tell everyone you're fine—but are you?

FUELING THE FLAME

To achieve something great in life, which the average person doesn't have, requires a fiery passion for that outcome to happen. You must want it so bad that it's all you think about. Whenever I wasn't writing my book, I thought about what would come next: *What would be the next quote or statement? How would the sections be ordered?* Desire must also be met with action; this is where I suspect most people fail.

We must separate desire from wishing. Wishing is simply hoping something happens out of thin air. Desire is done with passion and action. When you have that fiery passion, set a goal and put your plan into motion. This is where the real work begins.

When the universe accepts that it has met an unstoppable force, it has no choice but to give you what you are asking for. The poor can become rich. The weak can become strong. The uneducated can become smart. The only person who can stand in your way is you.

If you know what you're worth and have the desire, my next

question is: Do you have the courage to do what you say you'll do? Do you have the persistence to do it every day until it comes true? But most importantly, what are you willing to give up in the process?

WHAT IF I DON'T DESERVE WHAT I DESIRE?

You do deserve what you desire, but unless you change how you feel about it, it will never become reality.

When I think back on my life, I can tell you what I didn't deserve: I didn't deserve to be bullied, I didn't deserve to watch my parents go to jail, and I didn't deserve to look at both of them lying in a hospital bed.

I could write a dissertation on all the circumstances in my life that I didn't deserve to have happen to me as a child. But at the end of the day, it was up to me to make my desires come true. It was up to me to break that generational burden. One question I'm still asking myself is: *How did I make it through those days?*

It is your responsibility to find that answer for yourself; many will search for it but never find it. But what I can tell you is that it is possible to overcome anything that life throws your way. *If you choose to survive opposition, then you will live braver than most.* You must believe that it can happen before it is possible.

LOOK FOR OPPORTUNITY

While I do believe in having patience and being in "the right place at the right time," you also need to know when to take advantage of opportunities. You can't always wait for the perfect opportunity before making a change in your life. Eventually, you must break the silence and take a chance. The first opportunity you need to look for is an audience.

So, I present you with a question: *Would you rather have a small audience and enjoy what you do, or have a big audience but not enjoy what you do?* Once you can answer that question, you have found an opportunity. If you want a big audience, look at what leaders and influencers are doing. If you want a small audience, then continue doing what makes you happy.

Now, that's not to say a small audience can't grow into a large one if you offer something unique that no one else has. When you can find that balance of bringing something special to the table while also doing what you love, that is when people change the world. Selecting your audience is also essential.

You need to find people who share your beliefs and then offer them something they want. If you share your beliefs with those who do not share your values, you will question your own. When I first decided to share my story, I created a PowerPoint presentation.

I showed the file to a couple of people, and then I offered to present it. Not everyone wanted to hear my story. I then put it aside for a while and focused on other priorities. But I wanted to share that story. So, I eventually came back and started to rewrite that PowerPoint into a book.

About fifty-five pages into writing the book, I started sharing my story once again. This time, I looked for a different audience. I found someone with a good outlook on life. But they also had a general interest in reporting people's stories. It was his job to write stories about what was happening in the area, but there hadn't been any good ones lately.

So, I saw an opportunity—and that is what you need to look for, too. Maybe you're not writing a book, and that is fine. Instead of finding a reporter, perhaps look for a club, a family member, a band, or even a friend with an open ear.

If you want to be great, you must sometimes give up good opportunities. If you're like me, you'll realize that sometimes "good" just isn't good enough anymore.

Maybe you're not looking for an audience yet. That is perfectly fine; everyone is at a different part of the journey. If you're restarting from scratch like I did, then I would say start looking for your mentors instead. Some people can make your journey memorable. *You can grow through the wise words from those who have walked the path before you.*

JOURNEY OF THE GOAL

The beginning of the journey will always be the most challenging part. You have to figure out where to start. You don't quite know what you're doing yet. You have no idea where the journey will take you. You have only questions with no answers. The goal may not even be the end state, but just the first step in the journey without you even realizing it.

One could argue that the first step won't be the hardest; the opposition that comes along the way will be. While opposition is indeed strenuous, as you progress in your adventure, you acquire more knowledge. When you start, you have nothing but the clothes on your back and a goal in your head. In that moment, you must be most courageous. You must accept that you will face villainous creatures, without any idea of how to slay them.

Maybe the villainous creature is *you* in your story. In that case, you must fight in that mighty battle with yourself. Accept yourself as the villain or choose to be a hero. On that journey, you will have to make many such decisions. Even the greatest heroes have to make dark choices. To control the dark, you must first find it inside yourself.

The more you confront it, the more power over the darkness you will harness. The further you are into accomplishing your goal, the brighter you will become. *You found the armor needed to shield you from your dark desires. You found a sword to fight whatever obstacle stands in your way and a horse to carry you when the weight of your decisions feels too heavy.*

Not everyone can come with you on your journey. Some will fall in battle, while others cannot keep up with the requirements set upon them. In the end, when you face the main villain, that is how people will remember you in your story. Who will you be? The brave man who fell to the sword? The noble one who sacrificed for the greater good? Or the fool who turned into the hero the world needed?

Reflective Question:
- Who is the villain in your story?

CHAPTER 6

ACTIONS REQUIRED

The perfect time to start will never come, because that time is right now.

A NECESSARY SACRIFICE

It's no secret that I am a fan of Jordan Peterson; I openly reference him and overlap with some of his ideas throughout this book. He recently posed a question that I felt would fit this section nicely: "If you have to make a sacrifice, what's the greatest possible sacrifice, and for the greatest possible good? That's the ultimate question of human life."

My answer was, "I believe the ultimate sacrifice is being able to show the world your most vulnerable moments in life. Then being able to take those moments and use them as tools to help others." It is the foundation of this book and why I chose to write it. Coincidentally, this was also the day after I wrote the section in Chapter 4 called "A Glimpse into Hell."

I could have left out Dr. Peterson's section and written my answer. No one would ever have known where my answer came from directly. But instead, I want to use it as a test of my book's faith. To have a mark showing the person I want to speak with in the future. Who better to talk to about sacrifice and adventure than the one who has studied it longer than I have been alive?

I aim to accomplish many ideas with this book. In a way, you will notice that it isn't just one book, but two different books entirely. There is a part of the book where I tell my personal story and am most vulnerable. Then there is the other part of the book, where I speak more directly to you and ask you to answer your own questions in life.

Giving you the ability to answer your own questions and adopt a softer tone will enable you to be open without being discouraged from continuing this journey. It should feel as if you're not actually reading this book alone but with a friend.

But why choose this sacrifice over any other? I could never have written this book and still have had a meaningful life. I could still impact lives as a Career Counselor and stay for the next eleven years. In fact, there are times when I wish I didn't have to write this book. But it is the sacrifice I have chosen.

What better way to honor God than to give you what he gave me? A second chance, redemption, but most importantly: a story to tell.

The stories we tell each other provide hope when we can find none left in ourselves. They are an answer to a question someone is searching for. You would be surprised by the difference one sentence can have in someone's life. Even the simplest difference of saying "morning" versus "good morning" can change the course of someone's day.

When I was around ten or twelve, someone delivered one of those exact lines. This was a time when my mother was still around. Our living conditions were not as bad back then, but I was still very quiet. It was nighttime. My mom was visiting my uncle and a couple of people who stayed with them.

My mother had me see an older lady she believed was psychic and who would read your palms. It wasn't until after the reading that I knew it was true. Even fifteen years later, I still remember the short phrase she spoke to me that day. As brief as six words, and yet it still haunts me:

You're alive, but you're not living.

Imagine saying that to a child, and without knowing it, thoroughly reading that child's soul. What haunts me about that line is that I knew it was true. But it took me another ten years to actually take the implied advice. Life is full of these events, and most shrug them off as if they were nothing. Maybe she knew the impact it had on me, but it's sad sometimes when we never see the impact we have on people's lives until it is time to say goodbye.

This isn't just a book I'm writing; it's also me being the person I wish I could have talked to when I felt alone. To be anything less would be wasting the second chance at life I have been given. To truly feel what it means to be alive. Not ashamed of who I was, but proud of the person I became. The person that I must become for those living the same story.

One could argue that giving your life to a world that doesn't deserve it is not worth it. But I'm not so sure about that anymore. I don't even think there is any other greater purpose than to selflessly dedicate your life to helping others in a time of need. If it takes six years to save one life, but that person goes on to live another ten, I see no wrong in that.

Maybe they don't deserve another chance, but do any of us? Who are we to say who gets another chance and who should be put to death? It's a concept that I still battle with, knowing that no number of good deeds can get a man to Heaven. But I suppose that also means no deed is terrible enough not to be forgiven.

Sometimes I believe writing this book will be my salvation, but I know it is not true. It could go on to save a million lives and yet still not save the one who wrote it. It makes you wonder how many people thought they were working for God, only to find out at the final judgment that they were wrong.

I have faith and have developed an independent relationship with God. I'm still on my journey; the Bible that I was once resistant to has now been opened. But at some point, there was no Bible; someone had to become the story. That's what I'm searching for right now, a story of my own and the answers that I can no longer find in the dark.

I firmly believe that the Bible itself is still being written. In fact, it never stopped. Many people have argued that God is dead or that we lack the miracles that used to happen. We have become so blinded by the modern world that we can't see the miracles happening right in front of our faces.

But God is far from dead; he doesn't appear the same as he used to, or at least how we see him. Sight is the weakest form of faith, which is what everyone looks for. If that is how you find your faith, then yes, you won't be able to see him. He is not hiding. He reveals himself in the everyday stories we tell each other. The story of finding him in the third story of the hospital, while dressed in a white gown, contemplating life and death. The story of a child who was never supposed to be born. The story of a dog bite landing a millimeter away from a major artery. The tale of pushing death's time off by a couple more years.

A story about a boy going to war with a god, cursing his name every chance he had for everything going wrong in his life. But despite every word, he was still welcomed and praised with open arms.

A story about a man and his glimpse into Hell: trading his innocence for lust and attention.

A story about a lost child who found his way home.

WHY SHOULD YOU ACT NOW?

I don't know what you're going through in life right now. But I can give you some insight into why I'm writing this book now and not later. I could put this book aside, like many other projects I have started. But I told myself at the beginning of my deployment that I would write it. I also told myself this would be my last contract with the military.

When I joined the military, I only had the clothes on my back and a phone to call back home with. I am thankful for everything the military has done for me. It has provided stability, forced me out of isolation, and given me enough money to give me a start in life. In fact, being in the military has given me better living situations than some of my family members. I have an apartment, furniture, and a car.

I'm not leaving the military because I hate it or don't like my job. I am leaving the military for two reasons:

1. I want to do what I want to do and say what I want to say. The military's reliance on contracts would be a significant obstacle to overcome.
2. I do believe that this book marks a new chapter in my life. I don't want to just help people in the military; I want to help the world. I spoke about this earlier in the book. When looking for an opportunity, sometimes you have to let go of the good to make room for something great.

For the book itself, yes, I could attend more classes. I could improve my writing skills and deepen my understanding of psychological thought. The problem is that achieving some of my goals can take six or more years. I am still young and have just turned twenty-eight, but no one is promised tomorrow.

That is where my true answer comes from. While I feel I have time left in this world, others may not be so fortunate. I am still climbing the mountain that others have not yet started. So, it's a question I have to ask myself that I cannot answer: *I have time right now, but what about the people who need to hear the story? Do they still have time?*

For someone, right now, this could be their last attempt at living.

Reflective Question:
- Do you need to take action or *be patient, listen, and observe*?

(Answer it at the end of the section.)

WHAT MAKES SOMEONE SUCCESSFUL?

There are only two things you need to reach success, and each of them, most people already have. The first is your *mindset*, followed by an *action*. The problem is that most people don't know how to use both properly. Our mind is the most powerful tool we have as human beings. It is what sets us apart from the rest of the animal kingdom. However, misusing it makes many unsuccessful.

If you have a negative mindset, then you will always look for the negativity and fail to see the positive. If you believe in nothing, then that is what you shall receive. If you believe a goal is impossible, then you are probably right. *Your mindset is an accumulation of your values, beliefs, faith, and hope, which then fuels your thoughts and actions.*

Someone who is filled with faith, for example, will have more positive thoughts because they believe life will get better despite adverse events. This allows them to fuel the actions required to keep going. Take the opposite and fill the person with no faith. *There is no fuel, and without it, the engine can no longer run properly.* Before you can act, we must fuel your actions with the right mindset. Developing your mindset is not always easy, but the part I feel most people get stuck on is the action of doing.

Maybe you have a positive attitude, but if you don't back it up with the proper actions, it is useless. If you have faith that you will get in better shape, but you do nothing, then it will never happen; in fact, you will probably end up in worse shape than before. This goes back to the contrast between faith and hope from earlier.

The mindset is the vision of your goal, and the action is how you're going to achieve it. Your mind tells you that you want to lose five pounds. Your next step should be to start a diet and exercise plan. But your actions must match what the mind is telling you. If I want to lose weight but I act by eating more, I will experience the opposite effect.

Your actions will typically be more important than your mindset. You can have a poor attitude and still have a good outcome. But if you've been paying attention to the story, you'll know— that's what landed me in the hospital. Maybe not right now, but eventually your mind will influence your actions.

DO I BELIEVE IN THE GRIND MINDSET?

While I do believe there is a time to grind, there is also a time for rest. I disagree with the modern mindset of grinding your entire life away. You need to know when to get to work and when to take time to rest. If you do nothing but grind, eventually there will be nothing left.

Have you ever noticed how chefs sharpen their knives before they begin to cook? Cooking represents your grind, where the majority of your work needs to be done. But it is just as essential to sharpen your knife; otherwise, you will have a dull blade, which is represented by a lack of rest. If the knife is dull, you are taking away valuable time for your grind. A knife that only grinds will eventually become just a handle.

You need to balance your work with rest. Too much rest equals not enough work. Too much work and not enough rest leads to inefficient results.

CREATE A TEAM

Near the end of the book *Think and Grow Rich,* the author talks about a group of people the author thinks about. He puts himself at the head of the table and tells them what he wants from each of them as if they were sitting there with him. Among the men are the idols he relates to and looks up to.

In my own way, I've built a mentor team—my personal council—made up of those whose values, voices, and actions reflect the person I'm striving to become. The first part I need to figure out is how I will tell the story.

Will I muster up the courage to speak it to the masses on a stage? Will I continue to write it all down and let them figure it out for themselves? Maybe go with a more modern approach and start a stream where I can talk to people instead of giving a speech? One of my goals is to focus less on motivation and more on being a guide for the lost.

In exchange for this, I am willing to give up my current life that offers stability. While I do like my current living, I would much rather start investing my time in my future goals.

I am willing to accept humility; I understand that I will most likely not get it right the first time, and my story will not be for everyone.

I will give up control and instead give in to faith. What I am asking for is possible; it just hasn't been done yet. By giving up control, I will also accept that the timing is not up to me and that I must walk in faith, not trying to force an outcome, but allowing my council to guide me in the right direction.

Let me introduce you to my council.

MEMBER 1: JIM ROHN

He was the first speaker I started looking into, and the person who recommended the book *Think and Grow Rich*, so it is only fair to give him the first seat. What I want from him is philosophy. When I think of speeches and quotes, he is always the first to come to mind, so his philosophy is the most important thing I can gain from him. Now, while I did say what I want to do and what I'm willing to give up, I didn't put a monetary price on it. The first thing that comes to mind is $100,000, but maybe that is too small for the amount of change I wish to bring. A billion is too much for any one person to spend and is not appropriate for the line of work I want to pursue. The amount I will settle for is $1 million to start the goal off. Jim once said, "Set a goal to become a millionaire, for what it will make of you." *The money is not the important part; what you are worth to the world is.*

MEMBER 2: LES BROWN

Les comes from around the same time as Jim Rohn, but with a different style. In comparison, Jim was calmer and more easy-going. Les had much more spirit and speed in his speeches. What I want to gain is the spirit of Les's speaking as well as the flow of going from one idea to the next in an instant. Speed is something I have already started developing with briefs. The volume, however, is going to be a challenge; because I'm usually the quietest person in the room. It is not because I don't have anything to say; most of the time, I'm in a different world, and my ideas run on overdrive.

MEMBER 3: JORDAN PETERSON

Jordan is an educator for the modern world and a person who is willing to dig deep into the dark minds of others to help better the world. His education consists of, but is not limited to, a doctorate in clinical psychology, and he has taught at Harvard University. He is not afraid to speak his mind and back up his beliefs with his knowledge. He has also faced significant opposition and must stand up for his beliefs. What I aim to gain from Jordan is his knowledge. What better person to gain knowledge from than the person who seeks it in others?

MEMBER 4: DAVID GOGGINS

David is the last member of the council for now, but certainly not the least. This ordinary man who had many setbacks in life decided one day that nothing could hurt him anymore. He went from weighing three hundred pounds to being a top-tier athlete known for running ultramarathons, breaking pull-up records, and becoming a Navy SEAL. He achieved all three, which require extraordinary persistence and discipline—three times what most people never come close to doing. From him, I wish to gain persistence—a skill that takes years to develop and keeps most people from achieving their desires.

> Reflective Question:
> - Who are the members of your council, and why have you chosen them?

BE PATIENT, LISTEN, AND OBSERVE

Everyone has an opinion in today's world, and one of mine is that we should hold back on sharing everything we think right away. Take the time to listen to what people are saying and observe what is happening around you. While other people talk about everyone else, we can gather information to take with us.

I spend time talking to people and listening to their problems, and by using this method, I can make predictions about who they are in the world. *Listening tells you what they did, and observing tells you what they will do.*

Other people will guide you to "strike" now. While yes, sometimes that is correct, researching and preparing are just as important. The actions you take will depend on context.

For example, when you are looking for your purpose in life, I don't want you to rush into it; instead, be patient, listen, and observe. The way you know you're on the right path is when you can no longer remain patient. *When you have waited so long that if you do anything else you won't be satisfied, then you can accomplish whatever you set out to do.*

Yes, you should tell your story through your mindset and actions. But first, listen, observe, and be patient—because not every moment is yours to speak. But when it is ... speak boldly.

Reflective Question:
- When do you need to remain silent, and when do you need to speak?

PROTECT YOUR DREAMS

It is your dream; you must believe in it before anybody else does. You then need to protect that dream. *If you share it with everyone else, then it will no longer be just yours.* If you share your dream with the wrong person, they'll convince you it's impossible.

You don't need to tell everyone your dream until it is time to make your big reveal. When I wrote this book, I didn't tell everyone I was writing it. When people asked me about my plans after leaving the Army, I never mentioned that I wanted to write a book and make a difference in people's lives. I only told them enough for them to back away.

I told them I had other goals I was pursuing. If I told my fellow counselors that I would do something unconventional, that had no guarantee of making money, they would most likely urge me to be reasonable. But that's the thing: protecting your dreams isn't sensible.

You have to build up your confidence, know what you want to do in life, and take a chance. Sure, I may fail, but I have faith that my goal has already been achieved. That is what it takes to make dreams come true. *You have to dream about it so much that it becomes reality.*

Protect your dreams. If you do not, then your dream will become another opportunity stolen away by silence.

Reflective Question:
- Are you protecting your dreams? If so, how?

CHAPTER 7

THE TEST

No trial is complete without obstacles blocking the way.

REPEATED TEMPTATIONS

I was on the right path for the first time in my journey, but I was far from perfect. When I say, "the test," I'm not referring to you sitting down at school with a pen and paper. For some of you, perhaps that is your test. But for most of us, the test comes from the previous lessons we thought we had learned.

Think of this as the world's way of giving you your temptations. Do you slip back into that comfortable space you used to know? Just like every experience in life, at that moment you will have to make a choice.

You are the narrator of your own story. When the suffering is over, the question will become: *What story do you want to tell?*

We are the authors of our own story. But in this world, there are two editors: one is God, and the other is the Devil. We are the authors because we have been given free will. Neither God nor the Devil will choose for you. They will merely present you with the options. The author's job is to use their best judgment to figure out what is best for the book.

You will use both in the story; unfortunately, this is not optional. You can't have good without evil in this world. At the end of the day, it is only at the end of the story that you will know which side you have chosen. But just as I have described with the story of Job, the bets they make will be the test you are given.

You do not get to choose your test in life. Those are given to us, each one hand-picked based on our experiences in life. These are the chapters of your book you will talk about most. The forced paths that were put in front of us. Whether we succumb to temptation or overcome weakness, we choose the story we get to tell in the end.

The world works in ways we don't understand. We say God knows the past, present, and future, but it is the future part I believe we misunderstand. The future is merely revealed in the paths we take. Instead of the story already being destined before birth, it is actively written throughout our lives.

It is when we make a particular choice that our destiny finds us. It is how a road to Hell can turn into a path to redemption. God is waiting for you to make a choice. I believe that's the reason why we are all created to begin with. That is why God is on every journey with us. We are not the only ones learning from this experience.

When he came to earth as Jesus, he became one of us. But he was also subject to everything we go through. He felt pain and he was given temptation, but in those moments, he experienced what it meant to be human. There were moments when he could have turned back and even asked if there would be another way.

If even God himself is not free from tests and temptations,

then why should we be? He is the ultimate symbol of free will and sacrifice. Imagine seeing every cruelty of the world and still loving each person. To accept them not only at their best but also at their worst. To be able to love a friend who was going to betray you in the end.

Notice this part of the chapter is titled Repeated Temptations and not The Final Temptation. There will never be a final temptation until the end of the story. Temptations are repeated daily; you will actively fight them every day. You will have to choose each day to move forward or to go back.

I was given a multitude of tests in life, many of which I failed. It was when I failed at the most extreme times that my old habits changed. At times, I think I wanted to fail. Maybe deep down inside, I wanted to be threatened—the adrenaline of living life in its most extreme conditions. Better to feel something than nothing at all.

Sometimes, part of me wanted to get caught. It would have given me a reason to end my suffering in an endless cycle of torment. I can say with certainty that if I had been caught, I wouldn't be here today. It took me six years to build the courage to confront these feelings. To be open instead of continuing to hide the skeletons in the closet.

But even after I chose to live and move on, I still felt that loneliness. I still struggled for the next two to three years, fighting those same urges I had conquered. I never found myself in a situation as bad as before, though, so there was some progress. That's what you have to acknowledge when you're trying to make a change: progress over perfection.

Part of me was still desperate to find the love I was searching for in the dating realm. In 2020, we were in Germany for a rotation. This gave me enough time to focus on work rather than on my personal life. What helped here is that we were more locked down. When you are deployed with your unit, everyone is stacked on top of each other, quite literally.

When you're on a rotation, you live in quarters, not in housing or barracks. Usually, higher ranks in the Army are kept separate. Most bases will kick Soldiers out of the barracks once they reach the rank of Staff Sergeant. This is a structure built so that higher ranks don't fraternize with lower enlisted and so forth.

On rotations, depending on where you are located, everything is off the table. For the most part, they will pile everyone together. Your Platoon Sergeant, who has been in for ten plus years, can be right next to the brand new Private. This, in itself, can create issues down the road regarding order and discipline.

I saw a taste of that back in 2018 when I was still in the Scout Platoon in Korea. We had moved to a training location for the month to perform gunnery operations. This was set in the dead of winter, very cold, and we had snow on the ground. It was cold enough outside to get frostbite if you were not careful.

Winters in the Army are a whole new ball game; there's a big difference in waiting outside for a school bus or shoveling snow. Imagine you're coldest in the winter, but your boss says you're staying out there until the mission is done, which could be anywhere from an hour to a couple of weeks. Even with five layers of winter gear, the wind would still make its way to your skin.

A tradition in an armored unit was to sit in front of the M1 Abrahams' exhaust to keep warm. This system is hot enough to burn your skin. But in the dead of winter, it is just enough to keep you in a cycle of getting warm and the chill of winter coming back.

But one day out of the blue, our Platoon Sergeant had had enough of the antics going on in the quarters. He gave us no more than a couple of minutes to have all of our gear outside in the dead of winter. We didn't have on any of those winter layers either, just our OCP uniform. Everyone had grown too relaxed, and it was time to restore order.

While everyone shook in their boots, we all listened intently. We were to clean the room and reorganize it into sections. He also made it very clear that if he didn't like the results, we would repeat the cycle. But such is the way of the Army, and this type of thing wasn't always uncommon in a combat-focused job.

We had the same living conditions in Germany, but instead of one platoon, some rooms were divided into multiple sections, making matters worse. These quarters were also in rough condition; they were old World War II barracks. The only thing they had updated was probably the mold tucked away in different corners of the room.

There were about ten beds on each side of the room, with a dual-wall locker between them. Everyone had a bunkmate at the start. The room between the bunk and the locker was just wide enough to walk through. The lockers themselves were enough to store a couple of uniforms and maybe some hygiene items.

But there wasn't enough room for all our gear because we had to share the area. Under your bed, you would store your duffel bags' worth of gear. Your rucks wouldn't be able to fit in your area, so those would go on the outside walk area of the bed. This now constrains movement to walking, even within the building.

These beds were also not up to standard living conditions. Most people in the Army have back problems after sleeping on these beds for nine months. They are usually rough and springy. The bunks themselves were squeaky; whenever you moved, your bunkmate could feel it.

But all this description is to paint a picture of everything being constrained, which would somewhat help me. Back in the states, I could get away with anything because we were in separate rooms. Any action you took out here was seen or monitored by your fellow battle buddies.

But it is during these rotations that your coworkers turn into your family. You're away from your family at separate times. Now the only bonds you have are between the person to your left and the person to your right. One of the fond memories of rotation will always be the bonding during games like Spades or One Night Werewolf, where teammates' trust was tested.

Bonding would distract me from the desperation of being alone. One of the aspects I always hated about rotations was that each time I went back home, no one was there. It is one of the worst feelings in the world—getting back to base, watching the people you've bonded with be welcomed by their wives and families.

Not that I hated them for having a family, but it reminded me of what I didn't have. It's usually a feeling that hits home for many service members. The primary reason we have what's called redeployment training is to warn of the feeling I just described. It's the time we are most vulnerable to people taking their lives.

I'm sure you're aware 2020 was the year of COVID-19. When that happened, we had to move to new barracks, and we were not allowed to be stacked on top of each other. While it brought a great sense of freedom to everyone, it always came with its share of troubles.

With freedom back, so came the choice of secret desperation. It didn't take too much longer for me to find myself back in the old ways. The dating apps had been restored and were back to all the premium services. If I got rejected by all Americans, maybe my luck would change in Germany. But not much had changed.

While I found some temporary companionship, it didn't last long. With COVID-19, everything was locked down. We couldn't even get onto the main post to get supplies. It was work, eat, sleep, repeat until the policies were less strict toward the end. The closer I got to coming home, the worse my desperation became, dreading the feeling of coming home alone once again.

But hey, in the previous chapter, I told you I found my purpose again by setting a goal to become a Career Counselor. There must have been something positive going on to help distract from that feeling, right? At this point, I had completed my six months as a Retention NCO, earned a training certificate while in Germany, and was even planning a school date.

But fate had another plan that day: I was missing one thing to get my school date—I was still a Sergeant with no promotable status. Being a part of the training room, I got to see the people up for promotions. I was excited that month because I knew my name was on the list. I had been working on this rotation for just this one month.

Regarding my command team, I even told them about my goal to become a Career Counselor. They were on board the entire time with me. The Career Counselor with whom I had been working, also wanted to send me to the course. I went to turn in the promotion papers for the month, and there was my name on them. But there was one problem: Next to my name was a "no."

At that moment, my entire plan for the year was shattered.

I went to ask my First Seargent (1SG) why he denied my promotion status afterward. The reason he highlighted "no" was that he wanted me to return to the Scout Platoon. The training room was a temporary duty for me at the time. What that did was take me away from the team leader time as a scout, even though I still had Soldiers under me.

But because I didn't serve the time as a scout, he wouldn't give me the credit needed to achieve promotable status. I would go on to counter the argument, saying that I was in the process of changing my job. After the fifth time of asking, I had given up. I had no choice but to accept that I had to go back to being a scout.

I was back to the same person I had been running from for a year now—desperate, alone, and going back to the job that I hated. I had run a full lap only to realize I was on the same track I had been on before. The world has a funny way of repeating lessons to see if you learned.

I thought I had passed, only to find myself in the seat once again getting ready to take another test. Submitting myself to the hospital was just the pre-test; the real test had just begun.

But with every test comes an opportunity to make a different choice. I could accept that this was just how my life was going to be, or I could look for a different story to tell.

We got back from our deployment to Germany in the spring of 2020. During that time, I quit using dating apps for a couple of months. Two significant events were taking place: I had to leave the barracks, and that required me to get my first vehicle. It was a brand new 2020 Jeep Wrangler with a bikini blue exterior.

This was my first time making decisions and living on my own. I believe this is what helped me get away from the scamming. While freedom was my downfall before, this time I wasn't absent from paying bills. For those who have never experienced the military finance system, it's far from perfect.

I was still a Sergeant at the time, so I had to get off-post authorization to have them swap my payments because our barracks were too small to fit all the people we had. The problem was, for the first two months, they didn't swap my payments.

While I had thousands of dollars in new responsibilities, I was not getting paid for them. This led to my bank account getting nearly zeroed out.

I had an entire five dollars left in my bank account. I didn't have a credit card at the time, so once that money was gone, it was over. I had even blown through my savings. It forced me to stop spending all my money on dating. It was during that time of having no money or backup plan that I eventually weaned myself off dating websites.

While yes, I still fell for the occasional loneliness trap of sending people money, it was nothing compared to before. Instead of sending upward of a couple thousand, I'd now send at most a hundred dollars and give up on them. After getting scammed for one year straight, you tend to develop an instinct for when it starts to happen again.

Combine that with having financial responsibility, and it's ultimately what got me to change. Instead of feeling desperate, I got to the point where I canceled all the premium fees. I went barebones, which also put a limit on what came my way. I had found some online friends as well, with one of them turning into a short relationship, but that will be for another chapter.

What really got me off the dating websites was the repeated temptation from my darkest moment in the book. At this point, I had nearly given up on dating apps, but I would get the occasional match. Just like before, it was a standard profile. So once again, we exchanged numbers and began a conversation.

In a near-identical scenario, the age scam was put into full motion. But what was different was how I handled the situation. As soon as they gave away that they were underage, I told them I wanted nothing to do with the conversation. They continued to push further and sent an explicit photo. I blocked them.

The next day, I got a call. They presented the same kind of

scenario as in 2019: The daughter had been sent to the hospital, but instead of a father figure, there was an investigating officer on the phone. At first, my heart sank, and I thought to myself, *Why is this happening again?*

But the more I let them talk, the more confident I became in the conversation. The first thing they tried to get me for was not reporting the profile. Sure, you got me, but what the scam profiles will do is delete themselves after you match them, so they are untraceable. Strike one for the scammers.

Then, they tried to say that I continued the conversation. While yes, this was true, I explained that I would refuse any further interactions and that if they continued to bother me, I would report it. I also explained that I blocked their number and kept photographic proof, just in case something came up—strike two for the scammers.

The last issue that sealed the coffin was that they claimed to be an investigating officer working with the police. It was toward the end of the conversation when they asked for my address so they could arrest me. That was when it dawned on me it wasn't real. If they'd had any affiliation with law enforcement, they wouldn't have made a call; they would have come to me directly. Strike three, you're out.

It was after the third sign that I ended our conversation. I blatantly called them out as a scam. I told them that this was identical to a scam I had been in before. If they were ever to call again, then I would push them into an investigation myself. I immediately hung up the phone, and it was the last time I ever heard from them.

That they never called me back unlocked something in me, too. It freed me from my previous occurrence of the story. I often wonder if the same people who scammed me the year before found me once again. While I still don't have any exact answers—and by all means, the first one could still be real—it helped me come to terms with the idea that it may not have been. But again, what I did was wrong. I don't want this to sound like an excuse; my part in it remains.

My reintegration with the Scout Platoon had also been going well. Germany had been a much-needed break away from them. Even though I didn't like being a scout, I still enjoyed most of the people I was with there. They were still family to me. Half the time, I didn't really stay around the scouts at this point in my career.

My return to the Scout Platoon was short-lived. I had only been back for maybe a month or two before I left once again. This time, it would be a permanent move. I found a couple of mentors along the way who helped me make that transition. The first one helped me through my deployment; he was my Career Counselor at the time. I would frequently look to him for advice.

He left me with a piece of advice, though, that would shape how I conduct myself as a Career Counselor: "The mission would make itself. Never persuade a Soldier to stay in the military; instead, let them make their own choices." When my journey was delayed, he also connected me with my next mentor.

She was the one who welcomed me into the world of career counseling. She was the Senior Career Counselor at the time, overseeing all the other units. As my old Career Counselor was preparing to leave, he told me about a competition called Retention NCO of the Year that could get me a school seat.

In October 2020, I went to that competition. I was the only person to volunteer to compete that year. The only person who could stand in my way was me. I was nervous from start to finish, and afterward, it had looked like I just got out of a sauna. But most importantly. I passed the board. That was the first meaningful thing I had ever done in my life. It was also the first award I got in the Army.

A plaque still sits in my office, reminding me of that win. What happened next surprised me. My new mentor asked me to take on a vacant role until the next Career Counselor arrived. My packet for the Career Counselor course was submitted shortly after.

What made this special is that she treated me as if I were already a Career Counselor. I attended any possible training sessions. Whenever the program offered a trip, she invited me. She even invited me to Thanksgiving once, since my family lived across the country at the time. My mentor didn't just treat me like a Soldier; she treated me as a member of her family.

There were still plenty of tests to pass before I became a Career Counselor. The difference was that anytime something bad happened from here on out, I could tell myself one thing to keep me going.

I was going to be a Career Counselor.

WHAT YOU DON'T ALWAYS NEED

You don't always need a great start to life to be successful. Many people started with nothing and, instead of taking pity on themselves, challenged the world. You don't always need a college education; while it helps in the digital world, it is not always necessary. Now, if you want to be a doctor, I'm sorry to tell you, but you will need to attend school.

If someone goes to school and gets an education, it doesn't always mean they are smarter than you are, either. See past the disadvantages that have been given to you in your life and figure out where to gain your advantages. How do you beat someone who had a better start to life, who received a free education and has had more opportunities than you?

The answer is that, despite not having had those opportunities, you are still here at this very moment—which is something they might not understand. These opportunities in life have given them a good start, but what happens when they enter the real world? They have been protected their entire life, and so when life gets hard, they don't always know what to do.

But for those who started with nothing, they know that the only thing to do when you are at the bottom is to climb up; if you fall, you are where you started. But if you're on top of the mountain and have lived your entire life up there, I would make a bet that you don't know how to climb back up if you're knocked down. Always remember that if you play your cards right, *yesterday's disadvantage can be tomorrow's advantage.*

Reflective Question:
- What started as a disadvantage and turned into an advantage?

QUIT PREDICTING THE FUTURE

Recently, while on deployment, I was in an argument with a coworker. I felt like I was being targeted and he was out to get me. This bothered me quite a bit. I'm usually a pretty calm person, but I think this reminded me of when I was younger, getting bullied, and maybe it struck a nerve.

Now that I'm looking back at everything, he was only trying to make sure everyone was doing the right thing and making sure no one was overstepping their boundaries. It was the afternoon, and I had received a message from him saying, "Call me when you can." Although that was a standard text message, I immediately fell into a negative mindset.

I thought, *Here he is again, coming at me, about to target me for something else.* For the next twenty to thirty minutes, I became increasingly enraged and thought about how, if he did say something, I would be ready to take him down. I finally got back to him that afternoon, shortly after, and all he wanted me to tell me was that he was assisting someone I knew.

I had overreacted in my mind for half an hour, while he was actually helping me out. But here's the thing: Say it *was* something negative, and I thought, *I knew it; he just wants to watch me fail.* By predicting something that has yet to come, we develop a confirmation bias. It's what keeps many people from being happy in life. Sometimes *we are blinded by negativity and can't see what is really in front of us.*

> Reflective Question:
> - What biases have you developed through past experiences in your life?

ARE YOU READY?

Being ready isn't the important part, though. It is the act of being chosen and stepping up to the role. Maybe it's knowledge, perhaps experience, or you're not cut out to be a leader. There are hundreds of excuses as to why you are not ready. *When you are most afraid of making a change, that is the perfect time to start.* You must face adversity head-on and take one step at a time. One step—just asking yourself one question—is all it takes to start.

Now, be aware: You will fail. Accept that and continue moving forward. Not only will you fail, but you are expected to fail. There is nothing in life where one person gets everything right without making a mistake. When this does happen, instead of focusing on all the negative outcomes of the failure, recognize what you did right.

Maybe you wanted to lose five pounds in a week. But at the end of the week, you only lost three pounds. Most people stop right there; they don't see the ideal results, so they go back to their old routines. Yes, you failed your goal of losing five pounds. But if you lost three pounds, you still made 60 percent of your goal. So, why do we focus on the 40 percent failure when we achieved more than half of our goal? Before you started reading this book, maybe you didn't even have a goal. You have to take the small wins before you achieve a massive victory.

Reflective Question:
- Are you ready? Why or why not?

YOU WILL BE TESTED

When you choose to change your mind, you need to understand that it will come at a price. The world will race at you and ask if you want to do this. While writing this book, I was still in the Army. I decided, toward the last year of my contract, that I wanted to pursue writing and that I would have to leave the military to achieve my next set of goals.

Almost weekly, someone would randomly come up to ask me if I planned to stay in the military. I made my first significant career mistake because I couldn't focus fully. I was in last place—twenty-five of twenty-five and ten of ten—in my job, which had never happened before. The world wants to know how far you are willing to go.

Are you willing to do what you say you will, put in the work, and adapt? The test is not there to make your life worse, but to teach you something that you will need later down the road. The hard part is knowing that *you can pass the test and still not make it in this world. Sometimes the correct answer today is the wrong one tomorrow.*

REDEFINE FAILURE

We often see failure as something negative to avoid. But this is where we get things wrong. Failure is a key element to any task; a champion isn't born perfect, but he became number one because, instead of giving up after failure, he learned and adapted. I have failed my entire life, and yet I still wake up every morning. The next time you fail at something, I want you to think of these three questions.

Have you failed before? The answer is probably yes. Congratulations! You are not perfect, and you are a human being like the rest of us.

Did you improve? The answer to this is probably also yes; it's nearly impossible to get worse at something the more you practice.

Did you learn something? The answer to this should also be yes. If you have learned nothing and gained nothing, then you have truly failed and may want to rethink your strategy—or whether this is even something you genuinely want to pursue in life.

I ask these specific questions because they focus not on failure, but on progress.

IS FAILURE BAD?

Failure is a lesson that everyone must learn on the path to success. Quitting, however, is much different. *The only time failure is guaranteed is when you quit. Any other time, failure is not the predetermined outcome.*

So, ask yourself, "What if I fail?" If you don't do it, then you will fail automatically. By attempting to do whatever it is you say you will, you have increased your odds by 50 percent. Half the time you will fail; the other half, you will succeed.

So, by simply accepting the challenge, you have cut the odds of failure in half. If you make a routine, set a goal, and study, the odds are now in your favor.

Now, don't try to twist my words; some things you *should* quit. Maybe for you it's smoking or drinking. Everyone has their addictions, and there are healthy ways to stop them if you are determined to do so.

HOW MUCH DOES LUCK PLAY A ROLE IN THE STORY?

I tell my story because I don't want people to see my success and say, "You just got lucky." While luck does play a role, I believe it accounts for only a small percentage.

One of the hard questions I asked myself was, "What were the odds of my becoming successful in life based on my background?" With the significant advances of technology and artificial intelligence, I used ChatGPT to keep track of my sections of the book. After most of the book was written, I asked that question, and the odds came back at around 10–20 percent.

If I had known those odds beforehand, I might have said, "Why bother?" Well, here is the turning point. *Sometimes in life, you have to make your own luck.* The same principle applies to passing a challenging class, landing a dream job, or chasing an elite goal. Take any extreme example—special forces, professional sports, or medical school—and the odds are even lower. Yet, in every class, people make it.

Most people who have achieved their seemingly impossible goals would echo my suggestions: Their success had to do with hard work and maybe a tiny dash of luck. You need to remember that *it is not about the likelihood of passing or failing, but the percentage of energy a human being is willing to put into their journey.* In my opinion, luck will not get you any of these positions; it can only get you so far.

When I look at my 10–20 percent success rate, I see the *failure rate of those who gave up before me.* That percentage never had an impact on any of us. *You just have to be the one who's willing to do what others won't.*

MY FIRST HEARTBREAK

I have been broken four times in my life. The first break occurred in 2017 while I was in school to become a nurse, when I had my heart shattered by the first person I asked out on a date. It took me a long time to recover from this experience. I invested emotionally in this person and put everything out there just for a chance.

I remember the attraction came from her being different from everyone else—funny, but also not afraid to be herself. Other students bashed her, which is something I could relate to from throughout my life. Initially, I wanted to be friends and nothing more, but when I heard some people I knew had bad intentions toward her, I tried to get to her first.

Leading up to that day, she had told me she was missing home. She had missed some of her animals and had consistently talked about them. So, I used that information to help craft a way to ask her out. A couple of miles down the road, we had a mall with a Build-A-Bear workshop. I used the animals' descriptions to build something so she would have a part of her home with her.

One of the animals had a pocket where I slipped a note, asking her out later. I tried to do it discreetly because, at that time, dating had consequences. That was one of the reasons she rejected me. I had let it go for the day, but unfortunately, I later made things worse by not accepting the answer.

The next day, I tried once again, even though I already knew the response I would get. What made it worse was that I had to stand next to this person every day. That night, my hand was forced; I was told to stop, or I would get reported for harassment. I had hidden my feelings for years, but on that night, I bawled my eyes out.

The next day, I found out that everyone in that class, which was probably a hundred people, knew about what had happened. I tried to avoid her at all costs from that point forward. I switched my seats in the classroom, and if I saw her in public, I'd turn around. It's tough to overcome a rejection that you have to face every day.

Eventually, it was too much to keep up with, and I failed my exams and got kicked out of the course. I found out later that she passed the exams and became a nurse. I was still stuck at that location for a couple of months before they moved me to my next job. During those months, I was trapped in a pattern of sadness, grief, anger, and other negative emotions. I broke for the first time in my life. I found out my feelings were so strong that I couldn't hold them back anymore.

But I had to. If I didn't, then the situation would only get worse. So instead of confronting them face to face, I wrote them down. It didn't matter what time of day it was; if I had to let it out, I did. Sometimes it was at midnight, when everyone else was sleeping. I wrote all day, every day. What I wrote, of course, was how I felt about that person. The love I still wanted, the sadness of losing her, and the anger of being rejected filled the pages of my journal.

Unfortunately, I let someone hold onto that journal, and I never got it back. Maybe it's best to leave some of those memories behind. It unlocked a gift in me that I didn't know I had. Although it was one of the worst experiences of my life, it had produced some of the strongest emotions I had ever felt. I suppose that's how I know it was love. When everything inside tells you to try again, but you know you have to stay away, then you know.

Looking back, I realize she was not the problem. The problem was that I hadn't yet learned to accept rejection. All of this could have been avoided if I had just moved on with my life after the first attempt. The same could be said for the dating apps a couple of years down the road.

But sometimes we have to learn the hard way. It was another stepping stone in my story. The rejection was another lesson on self-love. Without it, I don't think you would be reading this book.

The loss of love and my nursing career sent me down a hard road to recovery. It's irony at its best; *the most painful moments on our journey end up being the best stories in the end.*

Reflective Question:
- What did you learn from your heartbreak that you still apply to relationships?

CHAPTER 8

REBUILDING YOUR CONFIDENCE

Broken by others, you are restored through belief in yourself.

FINDING SELF-LOVE

While my war with God ended in 2019, I didn't begin rebuilding my faith until 2021 and 2022. While I look back now to the events that led up to it, I didn't find God in my story at first. I had to restore the faith I'd lost in myself before I could believe in anything else. Perhaps I felt I needed to be worthy before I could make my peace with him.

Self-love was always the key piece I lacked in my puzzle. It was what created the desperation in looking for it in love for others. But it took me these two years to discover that it was missing. It's not that I couldn't confront the feelings, but I still hadn't known they existed until looking back at my story.

To write this book, I had to drag my mind back to Hell, the one I willingly created in the first place. That is why some of my stories and concepts are more extreme. I have to recreate the experience and, at the same time, apply my newfound faith to incorporate it for the reader. A tricky balancing act, to say the least.

It was after I had competed for the Retention NCO of the Year board that I felt self-love return. It was a rebirth—an event that showed me I was on the right path. Shortly after, we had a meeting with my current command team and the Senior Career Counselor on the next step. We had a different 1SG than the one who had prevented me from going to the promotion board before.

He was more open to letting me prove myself rather than to stay with the Scout Platoon. There was a vacant seat that needed a retention rep to cover down. Instead of the 1SG saying yes to me taking the seat, he left the decision to me while also addressing his concerns. I still didn't have the school seat at the time, so it was unknown how long I would be in the position.

He said that by taking this position, I would also be taking a massive risk in my Army career. If I made it to school and passed, it would work out. But if I didn't pass the course, I would be putting myself at an extreme disadvantage. I would be even further behind as a scout—not just by six months, but by years.

For me, it wasn't even an option; it was a risk I was willing to take. I had already invested over a year to get this far. I knew the consequences of not passing; failure was no longer an option.

My personal side of life was also looking up. I had started to find a time in my life where I was happy again. This had been absent in my life for years up to that point. One aspect of myself I always hated was how I looked. I had zero self-esteem and confidence before my life started to turn around in 2021. I started looking back at the culture I was raised in.

My father, for example, was heavily involved in the punk scene. Before I was old enough to remember, he had long hair, sometimes dyed a different color. He also had a long mohawk for a while that was at least a foot in length when standing up. He has gauges in his ears and is heavily tattooed from head to toe—no understatement.

While I grew up, he was mainly a factory worker. However, when I was young, he also briefly got into piercing and tattooing. Due to that, it was the culture I was frequently around. Back then, he was a pretty relaxed person, but if you judged him by his appearance, you would never have known. I think that happens quite often in the tattooing community, just a misunderstood group trying to live their life like everyone else.

I also want people to understand that my parents were never bad people; they just made a couple of bad decisions. In my teenage years, I noticed a shift in my father's mood. But after knowing some of his stories and emotional trauma, I can't say I blame him. I think when we are kids, we see our parents as heroes who can do no wrong. We don't see the whole picture of what is really behind the scenes until we're old enough to understand.

I enjoyed spending time with my father a lot when I was young. He would pick me up on weekends, and I stayed with my mother during the weekdays. The other thing he was always big on was biking—sometimes going ten miles or more—or hiking in the local parks. It was pretty standard for us to visit the local dollar theater to see a movie. This is where I discovered my love for horror movies.

I used to be a very timid and scared kid, even in the most basic interactions. Horror movies would be the worst; if I saw them on the screen, I would turn and run away. But I always heard a story from my family about a movie my father let me watch one day. To give you some context, when I was around four or five, my dad let me pick a movie. For some odd reason, I chose one called *Hellraiser*.

Later that night, I told my mom on the phone that I was scared of the man with pins in his head. Rationally, my mom was not very happy I had been allowed to watch the movie. But what that movie did when I was younger was pique my curiosity. Eventually, I worked my way up to watching it again. From that point on, I was hooked on the horror genre.

On April 13, 2021, I got my first tattoo. The same movie that scared me as a kid was the centerpiece adorned on my chest. To this day, a picture of Pinhead, a fictional demon that would drag people to Hell with chains, stares back at you when I take off my shirt. I put him in the center as another commitment to myself to continue with tattoos. Today, I have added several horror movie icons to the collection.

Sometimes it's weird what makes us happy in life. Even something that represents Hell can bring you back to the light. During this time, I was rediscovering faith. Maybe I was trying to figure out where I still belonged in this world. But we are the authors of the story, remember? The choices are up to us.

I have often thought about how the religious community would view these tattoos. Would they condemn me for still wearing them, or would they understand that you can find light even in the darkest of places? Even now, I don't think I would erase them from my body. If I did, then the one person I would erase them for would still know that they were there in the final judgment.

In my eyes, erasing them or covering them up means I am unable to live with the decisions I have made. I believe it's important not to try to erase your past, but to openly acknowledge what was going on at the time. The tattoo, while it represents Hell, is also part of my story.

Many will see a picture of Hell, but I see someone who has overcome it.

While that process was underway, I also found love for the very first time in my life. She was the first woman to accept me for who I was. I could be honest with her, and she could be honest with me. She was slightly taller than I and about the same weight. She was a couple of years younger and into the emo scene.

She had the same love for the horror scene. She had red hair, which, for some reason, I have always found attractive. It's most likely related to the bright color, which helps identify other people's musical tastes (metal, punk, rock).

The more I found out about her, the more she drew me in. At times, it was almost as if I were looking in a mirror. She came from a background that sounded worse than my own. She had just as many scars as I did, but hers were both mental and physical, showing on the body. I found someone who was just as broken as I was, but who had also accepted me.

This was a person I was ready to dedicate my life to. It was the part of me that had been missing, and I wanted to discover it with her. I had been alone for over twenty years, and finally, someone out there was for me.

We met on a horror game we both enjoyed playing. After a while, I was invited into her Discord and friend group. For a while, she was my best friend, which led to a romance; that had only made sense. In fact, it was when a friend of hers teased us about being too close that we became romantic.

She had just gotten out of a relationship, and we transitioned fast into ours. She wanted to keep this relationship private between us at the time, which I understood. All of her friends were male on that server, so that they could be a bit protective and judgmental. Looking back, however, this would be the most significant cause of our issues.

The more we tried to hide it, the more it became a challenge. The first problem was that every single person on that server wanted to date her. Making her dating life a secret gave each of them the chance to ask her out. She was a kind person, which made it very difficult for her to reject them—all while keeping us a secret.

Eventually, this became a problem with me, as well. I grew quite resentful, feeling that I wasn't good enough to be acknowledged as a partner. The hard part is that I felt like a third wheel, like she was willing to put everyone else before me. She spent most of the time on Discord or with her family. I would then have to stay on and message her separately.

We had no privacy or freedom, and no way to have a relationship other than a secret chain of messages. Eventually, even those private messages we sent to each other had been discovered. Out of nowhere, she had disappeared for over a week. She logged off of Discord, and even when I texted her back, she refused to respond.

When she came back, it took her a while to tell me what happened. The messages we were sending back and forth, supposed to be just for us, had been discovered. When she was out of the room, her sister went spying on her messages. Once that happened, all hell broke loose for her. The sister then took those messages to her mother, which sparked a huge fight.

It immediately created a divide in the relationship. I felt like I could no longer be intimate or romantic with the person I was dating. In a relationship, you are supposed to be able to talk to one another—but when she got angry, she would go ghost mode, which angered me more than anything else.

Our secret relationship would eventually turn into more secrets—only for me. But I continued in hopes of recovering what we'd initially had. I was back home around the holidays, and she lived in just the next town over. When we met for the first time, her friends were around.

I didn't mind because we all had a neutral relationship at the time. But everything still had to be hidden within plain sight. We had to make the most of the little time we did have—maybe thirty seconds on the way down the elevator—when we could actually hold each other. Those were the moments that meant the world to me, even as short as they were.

I believe in those moments she felt the same. We couldn't go anywhere alone unless it was in complete secrecy. I even wanted to go to her house to meet the family, maybe then we could fix what had been broken. But it was the holidays, and they wanted nothing to do with me. When I was able to be around her, it felt good.

The problem was that I was still stationed in Fort Hood, all the way on the other side of the United States. I do believe if I had been local, things would have worked out differently. As the miles grew between us, love faded just as quickly as a car driving down the road. Eventually, our relationship became quite toxic.

I felt increasingly resentful of having to hide, and in turn, I became a bully. While that was happening, I could see it a mile away: She was beginning to see someone else but trying to hide it. I knew it when she kicked me out of one of the groups and invited someone else in. A couple of days later, she told me.

It was one of her old relationships she wasn't over yet. She had never told me about it before, since she thought she had moved on. But the more I was away, the more he made his way back into her life. In that moment, I realized I had lost my best friend. I didn't respond very kindly.

I had made friends with her sister and mother again, who were on the server. I had erased all of them, which hurt the little sister more than anyone else. I felt pretty bad for that one. There was a lot of back-and-forth fighting from here. I tried to come back as a friend, but of course, that would never work out. I had too many feelings for her to be friends again. The more I held on, the worse it got.

I became so depressed at the time that my body began to shut down. I couldn't eat; my throat couldn't swallow the food I had chewed. I couldn't sleep with the thoughts that filled my head. I called her one night to pour my heart out one last time. We talked, and I thought that I had won her back—but the next morning, she shattered me.

After this incident, she blocked me from all devices. Her new boyfriend, the one she had left me for, reached out to me the same day. He essentially threatened my life and then my career, when he knew I worked for the Army. That was my one weakness, knowing that I was soon going to the Career Counselor course.

During that time when my heart was broken, I had fallen to my knees and said a prayer to God. Before then, it must have been over ten years since I had last spoken to God. But on that day, I had no other options left. In that moment, I asked for her to come back into my life. He had answered and delivered a couple of months later.

I was pretty vulnerable. I hadn't cried in years. My body had never shut itself down like that before. I hate that feeling to this day. I was in such rough condition that I didn't trust myself to be alone. I had gone down to stay with another friend who lived in Florida; it was a four-day weekend.

The ride down there is about twelve hours straight, and I did it twice to make sure I didn't have to be alone that weekend. Even after the trip, I was still hurting, but I had one thing going for me: the Career Counselor course. I had to push past the pain I was feeling and move on with my life.

But, as seen time and time again in the story, God sometimes works in mysterious ways. He gave me exactly what I asked for, and she returned a couple of days into that course.

It turns out she was going through it worse than I was. We apologized and then started connecting once again. The issue was that I was ready to change, but I don't think she was. She continued to hide me from everyone else in her life. But I could understand for a little while; the rest of her clan hated me by this point.

Through a series of events, I learned very quickly that they hated her just as much as they did me. Within a couple of months of my being gone, she told me exactly what had happened. Turns out she had gotten pregnant during that time. The baby had already passed. Maybe it was stress; I never asked about it too much.

Tensions became high with friends, family, and the father of her unborn child. She was abandoned and needed someone to talk to. I welcomed her back into my life, despite everything we had been through. Turns out she was on a trip to visit friends in the next city over. On one weekend, I went up to see her during my course.

I saw how much she was being bothered by the child's father. There was an evident obsession. I watched as he called her phone until she answered in the parking lot. He had called so much that the phone's battery drained. That day, it was just like Christmas once again. Together, we were fine—but when she left, life happened once again.

The next day, I had to return to the course, but tragedy wasn't done with her yet. One of her friends, whom she went to see in the same city, had taken his life. I tried to be there for her as much as I could, but I had to focus on school. I offered her everything, even the keys to my apartment in case she needed a place to stay.

As the course went on, I could see she was slipping into her old ways. By the end of the course, she had moved in with the same person she had left me for before. When that happened, I had to make one of the hardest decisions in my life.

I went to see her one last time, we got breakfast, and I knew the time was near. That dreadful moment when you realize that everything you have been planning is about to crumble before your eyes. When we were together, there was a certain spark, but on that occasion, it wasn't present. I dropped her off at the house before anyone else could see us.

I told her I couldn't do this anymore, that I was backing off. I knew if we kept this up, someone was going to get hurt. So, I let it be me.

I would continue to message her as a friend, sending her words of encouragement. Even though I left, the love was still there. Eventually, she stopped replying. Then, somewhere down the road, I was blocked from all contact. But I continued to send her the occasional message in hopes she would read it on her bad days, even if she never replied.

My prayers eventually changed for her. Instead of asking for her back, I prayed for God to help her find happiness, even if it wasn't with me.

Eventually, I understood God's message. He never gave her back to stay. He gave her back to help me let go and find the self-love I had lacked my entire life.

WHY MUST PEOPLE FALL?

I once saw a speech by Angelina Jolie that made me question why, out of all the people, I succeeded over someone who, across the world, works harder, is more brilliant, and deserves more. But they are stricken with war, poverty, and never have the opportunity to succeed. *My answer is that some must fall for others to rise.*

Some will never have a good life; some will suffer, while others will thrive. In that suffering, others may be inspired to rise. In my case, I had watched both of my parents suffer throughout their lives. A mother who lost her mom and her children fell into addiction. A father who was scared of his past struggled to hold all his emotions in while trying to make sure his son didn't end up like him.

A child who had never felt like he belonged to any group turned innocence into hatred. Those moments when I lost my mother, my father, and myself for a time changed me as a person. For a while, it was a bad change, but eventually I had to recognize that I wanted more in life. So, by seeing what could be, I was inspired to ask: *What if I want to do better?*

Reflective Question:
- What lessons have you learned from others' mistakes?

FEAR OF REJECTION

After being rejected most of my life, I eventually had to face it head on and ask myself, *What if I don't get rejected this time?* But that would be too easy for me to say and give minimal context. When you do get rejected—even when you wanted something—you can still have a good outcome. Many times in life, my rejections have led me to the path I felt I was always supposed to be on.

As a Career Counselor, this has happened a couple of times in the job field and led me to write this book instead of continuing down that path. The first time was for a competition in which I had placed well, but I did very poorly in the physical fitness portion. I then reached out to ask for help in that field, while also submitting my name for a new position. Although I showed significant improvement, I still did not secure that position.

I applied for another position at the 160th SOAR a couple of months later. I had increased my scores and become healthier. I was once again rejected. Fast-forward a year, and I had received a couple of job offers that showed they liked my potential. But here was the thing: By the time that happened, I had started dreaming about what else I could be doing.

I was also notified that I was about to be deployed, which I had been told wouldn't happen. Being rejected for those positions opened up the opportunity for me not to be stuck on a contract for a long time. It put a time crunch on my writing this book, as well, and using it as a chance to start over. By being deployed, I could pay my debt, and I found myself in a place where no distractions could keep me from writing.

Sometimes you have to lose out on something you want to discover what you are meant to be doing. As others would say, rejection is a form of divine protection. Maybe if I got one of those jobs, I wouldn't be writing this book. Perhaps I would have settled for staying in my current field of work for the next eleven years. It's hard in life to know why something negative has happened and not have the answer until a year down the road.

Which is why I would like to remind you of my original three-part philosophy. *Everything happens for a reason*, to give purpose to the questions we don't yet have the answers to. Sometimes, those questions can take a couple of years to answer. However, if you remain faithful, the answer will eventually be revealed. *Accept what has happened.* Accept that you have been rejected. Perhaps the answer will change in the future, but that remains to be determined. The last one, of course, is to *move on*. When I got rejected, I didn't keep feeling sorry for myself.

I improved, and as a result, they wanted me for the future. Now, whether you accept or decline, once it happens, is up to you. Continually pushing past rejection and failure has shaped the person you see today. I encourage every one of you to do the same. *Instead of letting the rejection bring you down to its level, let it inspire you to be the person you were always meant to be.*

HOW TO OVERCOME FEAR

The two fears that keep everyone from pursuing their purpose in life are the fear of failure and the fear of judgment. *I'm here to tell you that fear is not your enemy. Fear is a friend that is asking you to take the next step.*

Every time you face your fear, that fear will have less impact. Throughout my life, I have experienced both the fear of judgment and the fear of failure. Remember, I experienced both with the first woman I ever asked out in my life. Not only did she reject me, but she also was in the same class as me, so I had to sit there and face that rejection every day. Word spread quickly, so within twenty-four hours, about a hundred other people knew that I had been rejected.

My biggest fears had come to pass. But that was over eight years ago. I did not die from it, I did not have a heart attack, and it was not the last time I ever asked anyone out. Yes, I was embarrassed and heartbroken. But life went on, as it will with most of your fears, as well. *Take the risk, take that next step, regardless of the outcome—that's how you grow—not by avoiding fear, but by walking straight through it.*

BODY, SPIRIT, AND MIND

You must build up your body, spirit, and mind to change your way of being. Now, you don't have to build them in a particular order, but you will need all of them. The first one I went to work on was my mind.

My mind caused a lot of issues for me. It caused me to hide away from the world for the first twenty-two years of my life. Fear, stress, anxiety, and chronically overthinking every possible negative outcome that would happen to me—all these initially built the walls around my mind.

I figured if I locked everyone out, it would all disappear one day, but then I was left with the worst person of all: myself. *I built a self-made prison, and the funny part is that when you do that, you forget that you're the only one with the key to get out.* As I said before, when you have nothing, that is when you must believe in something.

That is where the spirit comes in. My mind told me no for twenty-two years, and I had to convince it that we were wrong without seeing the results. The most significant part of the spirit is having faith in yourself. Faith that there is something more to life than just being another burden to the world.

The last thing I built was my body. By the time I got here, I had already strengthened both my mind and spirit. So, building my body up was just a bonus. Instead of constant sugar, insufficient sleep, and fast food, I filled it with water, healthy meals, and adequate time for rest.

Building up my body was the final step for me before writing this book. Every week, I looked in the mirror and saw progress for the first time in my life. I was always a competitive person; it unlocked something in me. I started working out for two to three hours, five to six days a week, with no significant rest periods. It was then that I began to develop the idea for the book. Despite everything that had happened, I was still here, making progress on myself both mentally and physically.

The body was something I had resisted for many years, even though I had been in the military for eight years by this time. The reason is simple: Everyone always tried to force me into doing something I didn't want to do. But when I decided to do it on my own, there was no stopping me. *My mind built resilience, my spirit built faith, and my body built confidence.*

Reflective Question:
- Which area do you struggle with most, and why?

THE MOST IMPORTANT PERSON IN YOUR LIFE SHOULD BE YOU

I say again: The most important person in your life should be you. When I ask you to tell me a story about yourself, you should be the main character. Quit watching your life from the inside and start living it from the outside. Yes, people can tag along, but it is your story. In your story, the only actions you can control are your own.

The only person who can push you to keep going is you. *You may not choose everything that happens to you, but you must decide what you do about your circumstances.* This was the hardest lesson I had to teach myself in life. When you look at my darkest days, it was all about loneliness and self-hatred.

Even when I made it past that dark era, I found someone in this world I loved with all my heart. They reminded me of myself at times, and all I wanted to do was help them. But by doing that, I put myself in a vulnerable spot: I *needed* them. When we broke up, I could not sleep, I could not eat, and my entire body shut down.

That is when I realized that this was another lesson. It was trying to show me that the only person I needed was me. This was around the same time I went to the Career Counselor course. Despite that heartbreak, I passed the class, moved on with my life, and have not heard from the person since then. Yes, I still care very deeply for that person, but if I continued to wait on her, I would not be living my story.

If you are not the most important person, think of it this way: Do it for yourself. At the end of the day, *the only person who will always be there for you is you. Kids grow up, relationships can end, and parents will not be around forever.*

Reflective Question:
- What are the consequences of not being the most important person in your life?

CHAPTER 9

EVERYONE STRUGGLES

Opposition fights for control of your life.

RISING INSTABILITY

So far, I've talked about how my life began and summarized some of its significant events. What I have saved, up until this point, is where my childhood all started to shift. I could probably make an entire book out of this, but I will try my best to describe those sixteen moves in a couple of pages.

Everyone will struggle in life; it's hard to notice that it's not always our fault. When that happens, we look for who is to blame. Sometimes, it was when I went to war with God. Sometimes it was my parents' fault, who tried their best to raise me. But it wasn't until later in life that I knew they were also kids at some point with even worse issues than mine.

At some point in life, you're going to have to make a decision. To take ownership of your life, whether it was yours to carry or not. If you don't, then the cycle continues with you. You pass your misfortunes on to the next person in line.

As of the writing of this section, I am twenty-eight years old. Before joining the Army, I moved sixteen or seventeen times. If I include the Army, I have moved around thirty-one times. That is more moves than years I've been alive. There were plenty of things to blame my misfortunes on. The moment I moved on with life was when I chose to stop blaming the world and accept the hand I was dealt.

As a child, my parents were never together, except when I was too young to remember. Both were still a part of my life. As I've mentioned, my mom was the primary provider, and my dad took me on the weekends. Both of them were always hard workers and tried to take care of me as best as they could.

My mother was never ashamed of who she was, and she would let you know it. She was tiny compared to everyone else in the family, both in height and weight. She always put God first and would never miss the opportunity to drag me into church with her. She was intelligent and artistic, but she also was stubborn and had a temper.

To speak more about her artistry, the part I always remember about my mother is that when I was young, she tattooed a picture of me on her stomach with her own hands. Not only could you see my resemblance in the picture, but she did this upside down, and those who have had their stomach tattooed know that this is a hypersensitive area.

My father was the youngest and most rebellious of his family. As I grew up, he was the "cool parent," some would say. But even as an adult, he can still scare me. He is very calm; however, if you get him on a bad day, you had better run for the hills. I'll describe some of those times here; others, you already know about.

The first place of my childhood that I can remember was on Charles Street. It was a small apartment, just my mom and me. At this time, I should have been in preschool or kindergarten.

As I said, my dad would come around on the weekends and the holidays.

My dad's side of the family was huge into holidays when I was younger, and every holiday, there was a big family get-together. My father's side of the family is also substantial. To seat everyone would take up an entire house. A garage built for three to four vehicles still had issues fitting them all in.

My mother's side of the family was similar in numbers, but they didn't do as many family gatherings. For them, it was mainly on Christmas when we all got together. On both sides of the family, the grandfathers were not very present, and the grandmothers held most things together.

I have a lot of fond memories with my grandmothers. One of them raised me when I was young, and the other when I was older. Perhaps that is why when I was younger, I even made a nickname for my grandmother and called her Momo—just another mom with an *o* on it. On days I stayed at her apartment, it was a simpler time.

She was on the poor side but always had a lot of possessions—most people would probably call it "hoarding," never letting anything go. Her apartment was in a tiny town. It was located on the second floor. I remember it vividly. She had an open stairway and it terrified me. I climbed it like a ladder, clinging with both arms and legs, holding on for dear life, afraid I would fall straight through the spaces between the steps.

To this day, I'm still scared of heights, and yes, open stairs is still on that list. But it doesn't mean I never walked up them; in fact, I've walked up them quite often, and I even did it on a tower that was a hundred feet in the air. Fear itself is okay. Letting fear control you is not.

My favorite part of constantly going over there was that we would always watch *Scooby-Doo* together. Over the years, she had acquired every season and every movie—some on tape recordings with all the old cartoon ads, and the rest on DVD. She also had a large number of dolls, all kinds and sizes, probably a couple of hundred, to the point you could never have a clear path to walk.

Back to Charles Street, though, I don't have many specific memories of that place. I do remember my mom had a close childhood friend who also had kids, and we would visit them from time to time. When I went over there, I enjoyed myself gaming and jumping on their trampoline. Plus, they had dogs, which I have always had a weakness for.

I could never say no to petting a dog whenever I got the chance, and most dogs gravitated toward me throughout my childhood. The dog I liked most was Dexter, a Rottweiler who would always get excited when I visited.

The memories of Charles Street that I do have, I still hold on to. The first was at the laundromat. I was still young and knew nothing about the pay phones. Of course, I had an imagination, and I would run around keeping myself occupied. Through my make-believe travels, I ended up picking up one of those pay phones.

I dialed 911. As a kid, I had no idea that even if you didn't pay, the police would still receive the call. "Help police help," I said, or something along those lines, and then a couple of minutes later, they arrived. They started asking around to see if anyone had called, and at that time I was pretty worried. But I managed to get by without them knowing it was me.

Another was dancing with my mother to some music she was playing in the room. I was still young enough that I didn't have embarrassment about how others viewed me. But that was the last time I danced in my life that I can remember. Perhaps it's because no one ever showed me how.

But really, I know at some point in my childhood, I stopped being the cheerful and imaginative boy that I have fond memories of. Still, even as an adult, I don't dance—not at weddings, not at prom, not even at a club, which I rarely ever go to. Maybe that's part of growing up ... but I know that's not true.

At some point, I stopped being me and let the world tell me who I was. Hopefully, I can make peace with that part of me by the end of the story. I do sometimes wish I could go back and explore that time in my mind. A time when I felt my mother was happier and less dragged down by the weight of the world. A time when I had a pure heart and was unembarrassed by who I was.

Toward the end of our time at this apartment is where I would be introduced to my little brother's father. He had two kids of his own, a boy and a girl, who were a couple of years younger than I was. I would grow up with them for an extended period. During that time, I wasn't always very fond of them, and perhaps this is where some of that innocence starts to disappear.

This was also my first bad memory as a child. Before they had even moved in together, things had gotten a little violent, which I imagine, looking back at it, had to do with alcohol. I don't remember the context of the argument, but he ended up throwing a glass of water at my mother and me.

As a child, I did not really know what was going on. I started to cry, and my mother, at this point, was in full mama bear mode. They started screaming at each other, and if I remember correctly, my mom bumped it up a bit by throwing glass plates. I still wonder why my mom came back after this interaction.

Even as an adult, this didn't feel like an ideal situation to want to stay around for a child. What she saw in me was unknown; maybe it was the difficulty of raising a child alone, and some other motive I was too young to understand at the time.

But shortly after that, we were all together under one roof in Machesney Park, just right outside of Rockford. A couple of initial memories were that I was always a terrified kid; as you know, horror movies were something I would particularly try to avoid back then. To speak to how frightened I was as a kid, it didn't just extend to movies.

All of us had tricycles at the start, but the others moved to bicycles much sooner than I did. Even though they were years younger, they were braver than I was. Eventually, my father took the training wheels off one day and forced me to figure it out if I wanted to ride.

One day, I remember seeing part of the movie *Child's Play 3*—the scene where Chucky had just been thrown into a fan, getting chopped into pieces. Initially, I sat behind my mother and closed my eyes. Eventually, I watched the movie and developed a newfound appreciation for the horror genre.

My other initial memory was that I never defended myself, and any time someone was bothering me, I went to my mother. Now, with two younger kids around me who liked to get a little rough, their father had said, it was time for me to start defending myself. Eventually, I did, which made me realize a couple of things: one, I never knew my own strength; and two, I was very durable and had a high pain tolerance.

The other thing I quickly realized was that I didn't get along with people my age. I always gravitated toward adults or older kids. At the time, I was beginning first grade, but the kids I hung out with were much older—late elementary or maybe middle-school age.

I had to be tough around these guys; football was not hand-touch and definitely not toned down for me. Wrestling would also happen on the trampoline. I remember one time in the dead of winter when we were out there. My entire body was frozen, but yet there we were going at each other, not even wearing shoes.

Things took a turn, though, when they got me riled up that day; a neighborhood friend held me down, while the other started to provoke me by calling me names and racing around me, almost like holding a dog on a leash. He thought we were having fun, but that was a big mistake. He eventually let me go, and when he did, I let all my rage take over. I immediately went for the other and hit him square on the face, knocking a tooth out of his mouth.

I stayed there a while thinking about what had just gone down. Knowing that I could hurt someone when I really wanted to, I developed restraint when I could and held most of my emotions back.

Oddly enough, as rough as I was around them, when it came to school I was the exact opposite. Someone could make fun of me, and I'd stay mute, not defending myself. It was a defense mechanism that would eventually turn into the isolation I talk about throughout my journey.

I found out quickly that kids can be fierce. Shy, weird, and having the last name Fish were all factors that had not given me an excellent start to the world. I was an easy target for both boys and girls alike. The boys knew that I wouldn't do anything back to them, and the girls were verbally meaner.

I can still remember that two girls would make fun of me by singing "Swimming in the Deep Blue Sea." They did this while making faces at me that resembled fish. Their lips puckered, and their hands were at each side of their face, waving to make the motion of gills. I was left out of most groups, the last pick for any sport.

I was smart for my age, and I grew up pretty quickly. The first thing I noticed was that we were on the low-income side, which makes sense now, seeing that four kids were living under the same roof. The earliest memory I have of identifying that we were poor was on one of my birthdays. I received two books—and I liked to read, but not something you wanted to receive alone. They were picture books, as well, so they didn't last too long.

I also knew that our environment wasn't very stable. At night, I always had a hard time falling asleep. I hope the other kids didn't have the same issue. It wasn't uncommon for my mother to be yelling and shouting down the hallway. Sometimes, I wonder if I was the only one who heard it. It is for this reason that, today, I never raise my voice unless I have to.

I stayed in that location for about two years before we moved back into the Rockford area. Mila was the name of the street where we stayed for a couple of years. For a while, it was the same group; eventually, my grandmother would come to live with us on the second floor. But even though this was the most prominent place we had during my childhood, it also had some of the worst conditions.

In the Army, we have a place called NTC (National Training Center). It is where units go to see how proficient their team is as a whole. It is about a one-month event scheduled almost a year in advance—think of "playing Army" in real life. The "box" is where the test begins. NTC then sends its troops to take you out.

I can't overstate it when I say that they *will* win; it's not an option. They have trained so long that they haven't lost to a unit in decades. The conditions are a large desert in Fort Irwin, with temperatures that exceed one hundred degrees during the summer. There are no bathrooms or showers in the box.

The reason I'm telling you about NTC is that some of those conditions also occurred when I was growing up in this house. It's one thing to experience it as a field event; it's another to make it your home. I remember these conditions to this day, and they are very vivid.

While the conditions were not permanent, they left a lasting impression. Sometimes we didn't have hot water to take showers, which probably made me the smelly kid. For a couple of weeks, we didn't have a toilet. It was broken and wouldn't flush.

When that happened, we had to use plastic Walmart bags. Once you were done, you would tie it up to put it in a separate trash bag. To avoid having to do this, I would wait as long as possible—not hours, but days—until I couldn't hold back anymore. This is something I still do in the Army any time there's a field event. If there's no bathroom, my bowels will shut down for the first couple of days.

There was one time I got injured after getting off the bus. After we got it looked at in a doctor's office, the staff there called DCSF (child protective services). When they came to our house, though I'm not sure how, but we managed to pass the inspection.

This house is where the relationship between my mother and my brother's father would end. From there, she was on her own with two kids. We stayed for a couple more months, but we eventually got evicted from the house and were forced to move.

From here on out, the timeline will get a bit dicey. This is where the instability really kicked in, and I have a hard time remembering the exact order of events and locations. The next place I believe we went for a couple of days was my mother's friends' home on Charles Street. While it was temporary, I still counted it. Nothing bad happened here, but we didn't have a place of our own at this point.

The next place was in a trailer park, where our grandmother had lived down the road, and my brother's father lived on the other side. It was just my mom, brother, and me at this trailer. While living conditions were not excellent, I enjoyed that place a lot. I made a lot of friends out there; some were better influences than others.

The worst part of the living conditions was that the showers didn't always have hot water. When it came to having AC and heat, it was hit-or-miss. There were times when it was midsummer with no AC. When that happened, I wouldn't sleep much. I would toss and turn all night. My body would leave a pool of sweat on the bed that could make an image of me like a chalk outline form a crime scene. Cheap fans were the only savior at the time.

We also had a problem with ants; they would occasionally find their way to my bed. So, if the heat didn't get to me, the paranoia of not knowing whether it was sweat rolling down my body or an ant would keep me up. While I made friends who helped distract me from issues at home, even that wouldn't last forever.

One of them took it too far one day. He used a device to record himself making fun of my mother. After repeated attempts and multiple days, I eventually grabbed the system to make him quit. Turns out I accidentally snapped it in half while doing it. He took my flip phone, ran across the street, and threw it in one of the dumpsters.

I climbed into the dumpster to find my phone. By the time I got back, I was enraged; it had been years since I lost control, but I was ready to unleash a lot of pent-up anger. There was construction going on, and I saw a thin, marked piece of wood with a pink flag. It took it out of the ground and approached him once again.

As he saw me approaching, he asked me what I planned on

doing with that piece of wood. I told him I was getting ready to swing in the short term. As he began to say, "I wouldn't do..." I had already raised it in the air and thunderously hit his hand. Just one swing, but the sound of bone colliding with the wood was equivalent to when a baseball bat hits a fast ball.

Most people were actually thrilled that I did this. I wasn't the only person he had pissed off by this point. I got on the school bus, but within the first class, they pulled me out. He, of course, called the police to report the incident. But everything was dropped after the officer explained that both of us would go to jail if he pressed charges.

During that time, we had people living with us. We took the day off to go thrift shopping to cool down. It was a nice day. Eventually, a couple of weeks after that incident, the boy I hit and I apologized to each other; we were just friends who had pushed past too many boundaries.

By this time, I was also a bit of a bully myself in my teenage years. I think this is where some of my rage turned into hatred over time, but it's hard to tell when someone starts to shift in life. Shortly after, tragedy struck our family: Our grandmother, who was my mom's biggest support system, passed away.

Tragedy after tragedy would follow my mother from then on. It all hit her at once. She was enrolled in school but dropped out. My brother, when visiting his father down the road, was bitten by a pit bull that almost got hold of his jugular. Luckily, he survived, but that injury left him traumatized for a while.

As we were moving out of the trailer, my mother also had her share of misery. While loading items into a horse trailer, it fell on her finger. She had to be taken to the hospital for the amputation of that finger. We then moved to a farm where she had some horses. In exchange for living there, she would help around the farm.

Horses were her favorite animal. She had owned the horses while we were still in the trailer park and had gone to visit them whenever she got the chance. While she got even closer to them at the time, it only lasted a couple of months before we were on the move again.

The problem was that the farm owner would always leave his child with my mother. When that happened, he would cry nonstop; combine that with a lot of other issues, and it led to a swift move. From what I know, she also gave up those horses she cared so much about. But this time we had no place left to go.

For the next couple of days, we lived in a motel. I don't recall sleeping much. I had an air mattress that was deflating, and there were also loud snorers. From there, my aunt tried to step in to help with money and finding a new place to stay. Although my aunt advised my mother not to start over with friends, she went to move in with them.

We then moved to a farm in Belvidere with those friends of hers. They had been friends since my mother was a small child, and she trusted them very much. While they had enough space, it was still crowded. Altogether, we had eight people under one roof. But it was a welcoming home and a nice break in the story.

I would go on to work with the husband of my mother's friend. Sometimes, it was a roofing job; other times, it was cleaning out abandoned houses. I enjoyed that work, but one encounter made it very awkward.

One day, when we were gaming in the other room, the adults were off on the front porch. One of their kids smelled something weird. I probably shouldn't have commented, but I knew it was the smell of weed. While I didn't do drugs myself, I had been around them enough to put two and two together. After I said something, their kid went onto the porch to ask them who was smoking weed.

They busted open my door, screaming at me, acting like I was the issue. Maybe I was part of it, but I wasn't the one smoking it while kids were in the next room.

Meanwhile, my brother had developed some attachment issues. Every time my mother left, he would have a screaming fit. But I can't blame him; he knew anytime she did it was going to be a while. I feel bad for what I did to him, but I think it helped him in the long run. The next time he had a screaming fit and would not let my mother leave, I snatched him up. I took him to our room and blocked the door. I put him on the bed and put a chair in front of the door. Any time he got up, I dragged him back to the bed. He had tears running from his eyes and snot coming down his nose, and he was screaming for me to let him go.

He screamed so much that day that he started coughing, and you could hear it in his throat, cracking. We did that exchange for about an hour straight until he finally gave up and went to sleep. In hindsight, maybe this was for the best—to wean him off now before it gets worse. Maybe it prepared him for what was to come.

I eventually learned the reason we left the farm, a couple of years down the road. The money my aunt gave to my mother's friend had been used without her knowing. We left shortly after that and headed back to the other farm.

She stayed at that farm for a long time, but she no longer wanted us around the people. She eventually made the hard decision to give us up. I went to my grandmother's, and my brother went to his dad's. I can't imagine what was going on in my mother's head at this time. At one point in her life, her mother also had to give them up. It was a full circle, but this time she didn't have much left.

Going to my grandmother's house was probably the best thing that could have happened to me. I was happy there, and it was the home I needed when my parents were in unfavorable conditions. My father, at the time, was trying to restart his life, which only ended up messing him up even more.

Remember that calm person I told you he was? At this point in my life, I couldn't stand to be around him. He wasn't around too much, and I suppose that was for the best. There wasn't a single time I was with him back then when he didn't explode out of anger. It would come out of nowhere.

The worst part was that he wanted me to stay with him, but he knew he couldn't keep me. He lived a couple of hours away from my grandmother's. I believe he knew I didn't want to be with him, which made him more explosive. It got to the point where he was ready to exit my life for good. It was an awkward conversation. Imagine your father asking you if you would be better off without him.

I suppose the only thing that kept me going was my grandparents. I enjoyed being around them, playing rummy and solitaire with my grandfather, whom I hadn't known most of my life. My grandmother would also play solitaire and do jigsaw puzzles. When I stop down for Christmas, I still occasionally bring a puzzle for her to do.

She was still pretty active when I lived there; she cooked, cleaned, and helped take care of the grandchildren for my aunts who lived nearby. I enjoyed her cooking; my favorites were fried chicken and potatoes with cheese. Even the simplest meals—vegetables with a bit of salt—were good. She had always taken care of her children and even raised her grandchildren.

Sadly, she is no longer as active as she used to be. As I progressed in my Army career, time caught up with her. She is still alive, but she has had too many surgeries. She no longer lives by herself and is supported by her children. My grandfather passed away about a year into my being there.

As that started to happen, it was time for my next move; she could no longer keep up with the house. I was then sent to live with my aunt, back at Machesney Park, but it was short-lived. She was present throughout my life, and more on the strict side. But she welcomed me to her home, and I still go see her when I come home for the holidays.

I made a risky move when I first went over there. I dyed my hair blue without permission. She was strict enough to warn that if I wasn't careful, she would shave my head. But luckily, I happened to pick out a color she liked. She also still had one of her children living with her at the time.

We grew up together, and we often visited throughout my childhood when I was with my father. My cousin had a lot of pent-up anger as a child. I don't think he did it on purpose, but when I started living in the house, he began to take that rage out on me. It was only for about a week or two that we would have a series of arguments.

Mainly, I would blast my music; it was the only thing that kept me sane. My music let me escape from a world I didn't want to be part of. He busted open the door to the room. I still haven't had anyone yell as severely as he did. Not even the Drill Sergeants from Basic Training matched him.

He was louder than my music, which you could hear from outside the house. You could see his veins popping, and with that argument, I made a speedy decision. I knew that if he got in my face again, one of us, if not both of us, was going to the hospital that night. So, I walked away in silence.

Only I never went back. It was midsummer, but I felt so much rage that I didn't feel the heat. I started to walk back to my grandmother's house. I ran away from that home to another city entirely. Within three hours, I walked the streets of a dangerous town ten miles down the road, but I didn't care what happened to me at that point.

My father found me on the road about a block away from my grandmother's house. While he was angry, he also found it impressive that I had walked that far alone. At the time, my father was living at my grandmother's, in the basement, so I moved into the room where my grandfather had stayed.

But my father was going through rougher times than I was; I could hear him and his wife at the time screaming at each other. There was one time he got arrested for causing too much of a scene. Another time, I could see him getting into another explosive argument, and he started throwing everything in the garage.

When that happened, he didn't know it, but I ran away from home once again. This time, I headed back for the trailer park, another long hike. While no one stayed there, I at least knew some old friends I could hang out with. Luckily, my mother happened to be driving down the road and found me.

I didn't say I was running away; I just let her know I'd left after I saw my father having an outburst. I believe that was the last time my mother had a vehicle. Shortly after that, she got to the point where her pain medication addiction—the one I described at the beginning of this book—really started to kick into full swing. My father, during that time, found someone new and settled down.

While he was doing better, his explosive anger was still there. He wanted me to stay with him, and he picked me up to take me to his apartment. I had only been there for a couple of hours before I told him I didn't want to stay. After that, my father wanted nothing to do with me for a couple of weeks. Dad drove me back to my grandmother's.

Eventually, we came back to the same problem: I couldn't stay with my grandmother. In fact, the house was gone, and she stayed with my aunt, the one I had run away from. So, my father gave me no choice. "You're staying with me, whether you like it or not," he said. I was still going to school at the time, and I got off the bus after classes.

That's right, within a week or so of me staying there, we were back to where the story began. My mother was going through her issues with medication. My father was destroying our apartment. I was forced to go back with my aunt, which I didn't mind. I only stayed there for a short time before another one of my aunts offered for me to stay with her.

She and her husband have always been good to me. They gave me a spare bedroom and tried to provide me with privacy. It was a big house, but she had three kids at the time. So, it was pretty loud, but I rode out the rest of the time there until I left for the Army.

I do thank everyone who tried their best to raise me. It wasn't always perfect, and I was far from perfect myself. But at the end of the day, we tried, and they will always be my family.

WHAT GOT ME THROUGH THE HARD YEARS

This is a question I still have a hard time answering. I have a hard time identifying what helped me versus what hurt me. Some things I did were good for a time, but eventually they turned into bad habits. For example, I used to be a big gamer. It helped me stay off the streets, but I used it to think less about my actual life.

I used gaming as an escape. It eventually became an addiction. I hated real life so much that gaming was the only thing that made me happy. This is the root of most of my academic issues. *Instead of focusing on making my life better, I worked on my digital character.*

The more I escaped into that digital world, the more I

missed out on real experiences. Gaming isolated me from the world to the point where I couldn't hold everyday conversations. Perhaps gaming led to my struggles with dating, as well. I never went to parties, never went to a school dance, and never tried out for school sports. *I lived in a digital world that couldn't hurt me, and in exchange, I never had a real life.* Maybe it got me through my hard times, but it's a mistake I wish I had caught sooner.

Finding that escape in your life is essential. If only for just an hour a day, it is what will keep you going in those trying times. Focus your time on something you enjoy or are good at that also requires you to become a better person. Don't let it consume you, though. When you make your great escape, make sure you are ready for the real world.

But there was one person who was there for me when I needed someone most. As my life was falling apart, they helped me escape—if only for a couple of hours—but it made a difference in my mind. That person was my aunt, who helped me prepare physically for the Army. She had offered to help me at a family gathering and, to my surprise, followed through on her word.

Not that I didn't trust her, but my mind had been messed up for a while at this point. She took me to get clothes and shoes, and about once a week, she'd take me for a run. She was an ultramarathon runner—not fast—but she had the distance, which helped me run faster. Through that, I could then run ten miles before I could pass the Army two-mile time.

Unlike the digital world, this was a real-life experience that allowed me to escape my current situation. Despite not liking my hometown, she is still one of the reasons why I go back to visit. If you find one of these helpful people, consider yourself very lucky. People like her offer hope to the world.

She was not the only aunt in my life to help me out. Many provided a roof over my head while I struggled to find a steady life. The problem is that it felt like I was just being passed around to my family. Even though they helped me, I still felt trapped in that life. Being given temporary freedom from that life gave me hope.

MY BIGGEST STRUGGLE

My biggest struggle throughout my life, despite being an introvert, was constantly being alone—all the hatred I had for the world and myself resulted from my one true lack: self-love. On my unfortunate adventures to find love, I failed to see that the most important person to love is yourself.

I discovered that once you find self-love, you will never truly be alone again. But to see that, you must work through hatred and truly understand that it was misguided. *You never hated yourself, but you hated the situations that built the walls around your heart.*

LEARN YOUR CYCLES

You already know your good ones; they are what make you function properly, make you feel optimal, or give you that boost in your everyday life. If you're unsure of your good cycles, start by identifying what doesn't work for you and then build from there. Your destructive cycles are the ones we want to focus on.

I have a feeling that for many people, it's a case of procrastination. I told myself I would wake up early, write for an hour a day, and stop scrolling through social media.

So, what did I do? I dropped everything and said, "Tomorrow, this is it." I deleted half of my apps, set my alarm for 6:00 a.m., and decided I would stick to this strategy whether I liked it or not. On day one of a new approach, I usually stick to my word. The second day brings the struggle.

Maybe on that second day, you wake up early, but when the afternoon rolls around, you start watching a video, and then you look up to realize you missed your writing period. The next day, you hit the snooze button. We see this all the time in the world: "New year, new me"–but if you made the same promise to yourself last year and are still in the same position this year, what's going to change? When will you quit breaking the promises you make to yourself?

If you want to change, you're going to have to break that cycle and do what you're going to say you're going to do. *Quit breaking the promises you make to yourself and instead break the cycle.*

Reflective Question:
- What is the pattern in your cycles?

WHEN TO MOVE ON

What we often do in life is get comfortable. This is something I have also struggled with. Sometimes it's simple: We see ourselves in a bad situation, and it's easy to decide to move on. Other times, we feel good about what we are doing, and those are the most challenging times to move on from.

My current situation is just that. I enjoy my job, have a good reputation, and have received praise in my field. But deep down, I know my time is done, that I have outgrown my current field. If I stay too long, I will only grow resentful. A friend said many times that it is best to *give the minimal amount of time to get what you need.*

When you find out how to maximize results within the minimal amount of time, that's efficiency. That is the current point I am facing. While the time I have spent in the military has been great, and I used my current job to boost my mindset, I have learned that it was never about the job itself, but about what I learned along the way to get the job and the people who helped me.

But oddly enough, I have also been in bad situations that were hard to leave. You would think that it is easier to move away from a bad situation, but that's not always the case. Perhaps it is the fear of the unknown that stops us. Maybe we don't think we can do better, or perhaps it's blind hope that things will improve if we hold on.

Take that same friend of mine who went romantic for a while. Now, she did warn me before we started seeing each other that she had a habit of hurting people. Deep down inside, I feel part of the reason I stayed so long was that I saw part of myself in her. But it was an old version of me—the one I had left behind years ago—and I wanted to show her the light.

The hard lesson I had to learn in this experience is that *we cannot change anybody but ourselves.*

FORGIVE BUT DO NOT FORGET

Forgiveness is the key to letting go of regret and grudges. Forgiving yourself is just as necessary as forgiving those who have wronged you in the past. Previously, we spoke of accepting what happened to you and moving on. Forgiveness is how we take those steps—accepting the choices we make and the paths others have chosen for us.

For me, the hardest person to forgive was myself—the conversations never had, the opportunities never taken, and the experiences I threw away. When you let that all boil together for a couple of years, it leads to self-hatred, and believe me, those are the conversations with yourself you never want to have.

Eventually, I did forgive myself and everyone else who had made my life more difficult. What I did not do was forget the experience. I must remind myself daily of what I did; otherwise, nothing is keeping me from reverting to what I once was. The same goes for others; while I forgave them, I did not forget what they did or did not do.

One crucial thing in remembering is that you can identify signs of repetition. If a thief comes every night and steals five dollars from you, eventually you will catch him. But if all you do is forgive and choose to forget, don't be surprised when five dollars starts disappearing again.

THE SANDSTORM

One day, I realized what had happened after walking through a sandstorm. This wasn't your typical storm; winds were about forty-five miles an hour and would push you around if you were not careful. From the outside, you could hear it roaring and the buildings moving, and of course, there was sand everywhere. What was clear as day was now a cloud of sand.

The wind and sand made a combination that was almost like a grape shot, spitting out thousands of grains of sand at your body with a slight pain and irritation. But there I was, in short sleeves and shorts, walking down the road to the gym. It was a Monday; usually, on that day, it was packed, and getting a machine was nearly impossible.

But on that day, hardly anyone was there. Every machine was available without a wait. That day, I learned an important lesson. It was simple: Most people didn't want it bad enough to get through the storm, and those who did were rewarded. There are a lot of things in life that are not comfortable and that we don't want to do—but to those who do those hard things, everything will be given. Find your sandstorm and get walking.

CHAPTER 10

FINDING YOUR VOICE

Silence is no longer an option.

LOST IN SILENCE

In a Les Brown speech, he says, "The graveyard is the richest place on earth, because it is here that you will find all the hopes and dreams that were never fulfilled, the books that were never written, the songs that were never sung." While I agree that is where they remain, it is in silence that we lost them.

It took me decades to find my voice. I sat in silence even while speaking to others. I never showed them my true character. I lost that character myself—how was I supposed to share it with others? Even when I was admitted to the hospital, I found it for a couple of seconds, but silence was still in charge.

It was the reason that it took so long to change in the first place. I worked, ate, and even played in the silence. It was there that my darkest desires were formed, when I had no one to talk to. I had no one to protect me, and even when others advised me, their words fell on deaf ears.

It was when I realized that none of us is ever alone that silence was overcome.

I still remember that, at the beginning of writing this book, I was trapped by fear and silence. I slowly started introducing myself to the people around me; the more they were interested, the more I tested the boundaries. Even then, when I had the first version of the book done and wanted to present it, the task of showing them the introduction took days.

But by the second time, the fear was gone. Even now, I have spread the story further and further each month. During this time, I have narrowed it down to three aspects you will need to overcome silence: *courage, confidence,* and *belief.*

You would think telling someone to possess these three things would be simple, but that's far from the truth. They can take years to develop. Some people are born with them, and others have to be taught. For the unlucky few, you will have to teach them to yourself.

Belief is where most people will start. Even when you lack courage or confidence, belief must be found. Every dream or great idea that has been achieved started with a belief. Sometimes, belief happens before the idea is even ready to be spawned. That is precisely how this book came to be. I'm going to share one of my many secrets from my book with you.

As I talk to you about belief throughout this book, there is no greater example I can give you than this: I wrote the ending of my book at the beginning. Before the book even had its title and idea solidified, the end was written. Out of the entire book, it is the one statement that has never changed.

While every section of the book changed at some point, the ending never did. It is still one of my favorite parts of the book, and I hope you will enjoy it, too. I wrote it at the beginning of my current deployment to Kuwait. That's where the rest of the book was written, as well. When I wrote the ending, I found my belief in my project.

Though no one else knew I was working on the book, at just ten pages in, I committed myself to making it my last contract with the Army. It was a drastic move, but one that felt right. I needed to make sure I didn't give myself an out—a backup plan. To fully commit myself to what I believed in.

I had many people try to convince me to stay, but each time I listened, my belief grew stronger. After the first time, you're hesitant; they have made good arguments. But the part they never understood was that I already had those arguments with myself long before they did. I played the what-if game with myself more than anyone.

I could retire at forty, with only eleven more years left in my current job. It's a tempting offer, not having to fight for job security and having the stability I always lacked in my life. But maybe all that instability was building up for this one moment, knowing that I could give everything up and still be better off than where I started.

I'm not opposed to staying in the Army, but I need to know it won't interfere with the path I'm currently on. I even have a particular set of words I'm looking for to stay in the Army. I sent the original manuscript to over twenty people in my career field. Some are even influencers themselves. I did that strategically; I wanted them not only to invest in me as a Career Counselor but also in the project I put in front of them.

Whether they hop on the train is up to them. I understand it's unreasonable for me not to tell them this. But that's just it: If I tell them that's what it's going to take to keep me, it's pointless. I want them to believe in the project just as much as I do, but if I tell them that, it may not be true belief on their end. It is easy to believe in something once a project is shown to be popular, but it is not so easy when you have to be the first investor.

Confidence is a topic I've already discussed throughout the book, so I won't go back into it here. The tattoos helped me explore my body. The gym helped me build my body; every weight I pushed was a step toward confidence. Then, of course, the exploration of self-love and faith was the final step.

Confidence isn't learned; it's built through pushing past the boundaries you create in your head.

The final one and probably the toughest for most people is courage. Think of courage as the final step after you achieve belief and confidence. Once you find faith and trust, all you have to do is take the next step. But to be courageous, fear also must be present. Most courageous people are afraid; they have just done enough to silence their fear.

For most people, once they take the first step, they realize that the stories they told themselves were exaggerated. If you have ever been trapped in fear, when was the last time all of those fears actually came true? Even if they did come true, you faced them, which is the act of courage. People are more courageous than they think.

When I was still in the Scout Platoon, such an act occurred, and my fears were genuine. I was a newly promoted Sergeant at the time, and I knew I had no business being in that rank. I wasn't the only one who knew this, either. I had never taught a class to Soldiers at that point. So, they threw me into a random one that had been going on that day.

I had to break down an M240B weapon system and explain it in front of twenty people. The problem was that I had to teach it to the infantry, who already knew everything about this weapon. There was no hiding that I knew hardly anything about it.

But there I was right in front of everyone. Before I had even begun, my hands were shaking, my face had turned red, and I was sweating bullets. My voice was shaky and barely audible. My hands were shaky, too. I was shaking so bad you could see the weapon stand go back and forth.

I tried not to look at people, but that didn't go so well. I could see the other Sergeants in the background smiling and quietly laughing while spitting in their dip bottles. Eventually, I was able to disassemble and reassemble the weapon system. I knew I was a failure, my confidence at an all-time low. I remember that when I went to the back of the room, they even told me, "You suck, Fish." The problem is that they were right.

I was also a Master Driver, which means I had to teach Soldiers about military vehicles and test them on a drive. The problem was that I had never owned a car in my life. I had to sit there and teach people something I barely did. Luckily, there were other Master Drivers. While they were there, I watched them prepare.

I was just like a student cheating on a classmate's test. I would mimic their actions and then use their teaching style to copy and paste over my own. I did this several times throughout my Master Driver journey. The only time I was actually decent was for a vehicle called the JLTV (Joint Lightweight Tactical Vehicle), in which I was given a formal class to teach hundreds of people. Even then, I stole a lot of knowledge from senior leaders.

I am always afraid of presenting, but I do it afraid. Most people can't tell as much anymore. Over time, it becomes a habit, you learn to do it so well that it comes out of your mouth regardless of how you feel. When it comes to any of the three aspects, I'm sorry to be the bearer of bad news. The only way to become proficient in each category is by actively doing them while not being comfortable. Courage faces fear, confidence is built through repetition of doing something you're not good at, and belief is accepting truth which is often uncomfortable.

Toward the end of my deployment in Kuwait, I had finished my manuscript and was waiting for a publication contract. But there was still one demon left to conquer: speaking about my book in front of others. I had been setting this up for months now, after it had gotten pushed back a couple of times.

It was nearly the same PowerPoint that had been rejected the previous year for presentation. But this time I had a book to back up my beliefs. My current Command Sergeant Major gave me the chance I was looking for. He didn't have to; even I saw the risk in presenting this speech to the masses. It was a class for suicide awareness, only instead of doing your typical military PowerPoint, I chose to discuss Chapter 1 of my book.

This was the first attempt I had made to make an impact on the public. To practice, I would review my slides two to three times a day. Any time I stumbled too severely, I would start over. This wasn't a short presentation; it started as thirty minutes, but after refining my speech, it's now around twenty minutes.

Initially, it was going to be done in front of around thirty people. But it turned into something much bigger than I'd planned. We had a theater that housed around two hundred people. I was nervous, but I knew silence was no longer an option. I had come too far to back down now. There were multiple lines I said to myself to help me find my courage.

They need to hear the story.

Fear is not the enemy; it is a friend asking you to take the next step.

But the one that did it for me was in the form of a prayer: "Here am I, send me," words from a verse I once heard in the Bible that is one of my favorites. It wasn't just a prayer, but a pact with God. It was my time to go up next, and I was still sweating. But then, by accident, they skipped my class.

It gave me one last chance to calm my nerves. The next day, I knew I was up first. I arrived thirty minutes early to try a new method, which I have been using since then. A 1SG at the time was on the stage watching the troops fall in, and he saw me. He knew I was the first to be up, so he invited me up front.

Maybe this was another mysterious act of God in the story. As I watched everyone fall into line in front of me slowly over the next thirty minutes, I realized my fear was gone. I believe the act of being called up is what gets me. But with me being onstage already, there was nothing to call out; it was all on me. Even though the previous night I was shaking, that night, despite some technical difficulties, I went through without hesitation.

I have done this class on three other occasions. I discovered something that was added to the chapters afterward. After I presented that PowerPoint, I realized I was never alone. About two slides in, there is a section for group questions, one of them being: "Have you ever been blackmailed?" It's the reason I had to build up courage in the first place.

I can easily talk about my father's outburst and my mother's death. But opening up to share the story about myself was a game-changer. Every time I asked the group the question, though, I was never alone; in fact, there were usually at least five people raising their hands.

I thought maybe people would judge or shame me. But every person instead said, "Thank you for telling your story." I even had a couple of people who told me afterward that they'd gone through similar issues. That's where I find my courage to keep going, for those who need to know they're not alone. It was at that event that I learned something about my journey.

It's a story that everyone will want to hear, but no one wants to write.

SHARING, GIVING, PARASITES, AND THIEVES

In any situation, if a stranger gives you something, it is a *gift*. If you exchange gifts with them, it is *sharing*. If all they do is take without permission, then they are a thief, and if they gain something at the cost of your loss, then they are parasites. Do you agree? So why would you view those definitions differently when they are someone you love or care about?

Take it as you will, but if you find yourself dedicating your time and energy to a relationship and receiving nothing back, what is the difference between them and the thief? If you go to work and pay the bills while they sit at home, not contributing to the relationship, then what makes them different from the parasite? My answer is simple: There is no difference. If the shoes fit, wear them.

If you allow them to steal from you, then it must not be worth much, right? If someone stole your money, you would call for help, so why let someone steal your time? The funds can be returned, but your time will never be rewound. If someone is abusive in the relationship, and they stick around you, you often hear them say, "But I'm a good person."

Well, last time I checked, if I said my wife beats me on the weekends, but other than that, she's a good person, most people would give me a funny look. Now we can clearly see these abusive people have a problem, but so do you. *If you let people take advantage of you, then what does it say about you, other than you have low self-worth?*

If you were to leave them, you have nothing to lose. If you were to run away from the thief, you would have an opportunity to keep your money. *If you're the only person contributing to the relationship, then leaving has no consequences and only has the potential benefit of gaining what you lost in the first place.*

FINAL THOUGHTS ON SCAMMING

This is the topic I talk about most in the book because it scares the hell out of me. It is the one I regret the most. I did it out of my own free will. I can't blame my mother, father, or any other circumstance for what happened during 2019.

Yes, those people treated me terribly and scammed me for all I had. But at the end of the day, I allowed myself to be put in that situation. Even if I had mental issues at the time, scamming happens to even the brightest people in the world. Maybe I trust people too much, and the same could be said for others.

I could have prevented every circumstance that happened. But I didn't. I must live my entire life knowing that my actions come with consequences. That at any given time, those old habits can come back. While I have made peace with the situation, it is still hard to move on from this one.

Maybe by releasing this book to the world, I can free this burden from my mind. After all, the scamming is what led to the downfall of my past self. This book marks the next chapter of my life—not an ending, but a different story to tell.

But who would I be if I wrote a book about facing fears, regrets, and moving on but didn't follow my own rules? It wouldn't be fair for me not to show you that I am still figuring life out. As I told you before my story began, I do not glorify my actions, but I also will not hide them.

MY BEST DAY

It didn't come when I wrote the book. It didn't come when I had my best victory. *My best day came from the worst hour.*

The day was when I admitted myself to the hospital. The day I was ready to end my life but decided to give it one more shot. That thought had been spiraling in my head for months before I finally accepted help. I ran through every fictional story in my head before I made that decision.

It was in that moment that I had silenced fear for the first time. While I knew I was struggling, very few people were able to piece together that I had been struggling not for mere months, but for years.

Through that one courageous act, I was able to find my voice. The same voice you see today in this book. While it was still quiet on my actual issues, it was the first step in making my recovery.

Enjoy the experience—not just the victory, but also the suffering.

When you begin to change your mind, it's not fun at all. In fact, it sucks—a lot. But once you've made it through, once you've achieved your goal and begin to reflect, you'll realize those were the best moments of your life.

The struggle. The breakthroughs. The quiet victories no one saw but you.

These will become the stories you tell your friends, your family, even your children. The redemption you found. The dragons you slew. The days you almost gave up—but didn't.

Enjoy the moment, even if it hurts right now. This journey only comes once in a lifetime.

THE PUZZLE

Changing your mind is like putting together a puzzle.

The first thing you need to do is buy the puzzle, which is accepting the challenge regardless of what others say when you go to check out. Sometimes puzzles are given to us; regardless, it is up to you to solve the problem.

You then must sit down with yourself and open the box. It is in that moment you realize what you have signed up for. You are not looking at a simple "how to," but a complete reconstruction that comes with no instructions.

In that box, you will see thousands of pieces shattered; you may not even know what shattered them. Each one of those pieces represents a memory. Scattered, they make no sense, but in the end, it all comes together to paint a picture.

What the picture will be is the puzzle you have chosen to solve. Do not choose the puzzle that is easily solved in a day. Go for the puzzle that intimidates you most. It is in long-term gratification in which you will find the most rewards.

As a suggestion from someone who has solved their puzzle, I would advise you to start with the edges. They are the foundation or the framework. These pieces are easily identified with straight lines; every other piece, you will have to carefully select based on where you think it belongs.

My puzzle did not take a day, a month, or even a year to solve. It took between two and three years for me to put all my pieces together again. I wish you luck on your journey. I can help you with a couple of pieces, but the other nine hundred or so will be on you to put back together.

Reflective Question:
- What will you do if a piece no longer fits in your puzzle?

REMEMBER WHERE YOU CAME FROM

Remember what it was like to be in your shoes. You have to remember not only the good, but also the bad. The bad reminds you of what not to be and how you have grown into what you are today. The good is what kept you going, despite all those bad times.

Once you remember where you came from, you can figure out who you need to be for the next person on the same journey you were on. If you forget who you are, do not be surprised when people turn their backs on you for the same thing you once spoke against. Maybe it's easier that way, but in the end, if you want to make a change, *it starts with you.*

> Reflective Question:
> - What will you do differently than those who came before you?

FIND YOURSELF

Often on my journey, I hid myself from everyone in my life. I allowed them to see just a small percentage of the person I actually was. I would stay silent to avoid disagreeing with someone. I tried to remain neutral with everyone and, by doing so, not be my true self.

Maybe it goes back to my liking to help other people. But is it ever worth it to change a life at the cost of your own? I'm not so sure of that answer yet. Of course, there are times when we need to sacrifice our time to help others. But where do we draw the line?

It goes back to the concept of being the most important person in your life. Your story should be about you before you begin to help others. You first need to find your own voice. Find what makes you unique, what you bring to the table, and why they should listen to your advice.

The only person who can tell your story is you. If you tell no one, then there is no story. Just like the voice you have silenced, your story is now lost.

In finding yourself, this is a chance for a rebirth, a new character you have always wanted to create. The fool who set out for adventure. The hero who conquered self-doubt in the darkest moments. *Once you find yourself, no one can ever take that away from you. Silence the voices of others, so that you may hear your own once again.*

CHAPTER 11

CREATING A NEW CHARACTER

The struggles are not over yet, but you still must walk the path.

A NEED FOR CHANGE

Do not be afraid to start over in life. Change is there to help build better character. If anything, you should be more fearful of comfort; it is the silent killer of most dreams. There are dreams out there that could have changed the world, but people were too terrified of vulnerability. After reviewing this book, I found a change I was making without even knowing it.

Some of the changes were good, while others I let go of. But even so, a bad change could be the last piece required to reveal who you were meant to be. If I were to give any advice to a younger generation, it would be to figure out what you don't want to do in life. All too often, we get trapped by early investments only to find out years later that we were supposed to make a change.

We somehow grow comfortable in environments we were never supposed to stay in. While I'm not saying a simple life is wrong, it makes you wonder how much you left on the table. How much further could you have gone? How much more could you have achieved? It is often these types of thoughts that keep me awake at night.

I have started my life over three times, and now I'm going for number four within a span of nine years. How exciting, when you're able to look back on life and realize that your end goal turned out to be just the starting line. It is only now that I truly appreciate life and the mysteries it continues to provide me.

The first time I started over was in 2016 when I joined the Army. Back then, instability was a key part of my life. I never knew what tragedy would strike next. But sometimes within tragedy is where the light hides. In fact, it was at a time when my father was in his explosive moods that my Army journey began.

In the year 2014, my grades had been at an all-time low, and I had failed my very first class. It was honors geometry. I never understood the subject, so I often slept through class. I failed by only a couple of percentage points; maybe one day of paying attention would have saved me. But that failure set my father off that summer.

Any chance he got, he reminded me of failing that class. But I suppose I can't blame him, he was trying to protect me from repeating his same mistakes in life. He pressured me that year to find jobs to pay for the class I had to retake. He held onto this for a while, even into the fall season. He wouldn't pay for a driver's education test then, if I recall correctly.

The following year, he wouldn't let me choose any higher-level math classes because of that failure. While I never got a job the way he wanted, it instead turned into "Have you ever considered the military?" At the time, I said "sure" to get him off my back. My job applications never got accepted. Most of the time, I would take a picture and then later throw it away.

But he wasn't in the mood for my excuses anymore. Eventually, it turned into another yelling match, and he told me to get my stuff and took me down to the recruiter's office. I went along to keep him off my back. Lo and behold, I ended up liking what they said, plus this was an opportunity to get my dad to settle down.

Yet another one of many plans God made for my path.

Soon, I was enrolled in the Delayed Entry Program. They gave me a green shirt with the Army logo on the top right corner. It was part of our uniform for the training. Once a week, the recruiters would do physical training with the Soldiers to get them in shape for Basic Training. I enjoyed this time with them a lot; it helped keep my mind out of the gutter when everything else wasn't going as planned. I didn't like being around my family too much at the time, so in a way, it was a second family.

It gave me something to look forward to—a goal to escape the depressing city of Rockford, Illinois. Even the recruiters were able to use that to their advantage. They said the wars overseas were safer than the streets of Rockford and Chicago.

When looking back at what my recruiters said, one aspect scares even me and can't be ignored. The recruiter I tended to favor was a 68C nurse, the same one I had applied with when first joining. But my recruiter was actually a 19D, a Calvary Scout. My destiny was mocking me before I even realized it when I failed out of nursing school and became a scout.

Between the Army training and my aunt coming to pick me up for runs, it helped keep my sanity in a world of chaos. When I was living with my father, he got a call from school saying I was missing fifty assignments, a couple of months before graduation. While he was angry, it was the threat of being kicked out of the Army program and losing my aunt's run days that kicked me back into gear.

The Army ultimately saved me multiple times in my life without my knowing it. But I will say they also tipped the scales into my insanity as well. In 2019, I started over once again in the worst possible way. I was ready to end my life, which ultimately led to my salvation.

I hope most of you never have to get to this point in life. But as a tip, you have no other option but to make a change. If the hospital didn't fix me the first time, in my mind, I was signing my own death certificate. Regardless of the repeated cycle going on in my life, I continued my search. If I hit rock bottom, then up was the only place left to go.

Fast-forward another three years to 2022, and it was a year of big changes. Despite the heartbreak of the first woman who accepted me, this was the year I found God again. It was a complete restart to my life. I had broken the five-year cycle that haunted my past. This was the year when I found myself, too.

I became a Career Counselor, and I moved away from Fort Hood and being a scout. I joined my first team of Career Counselors in October of 2022. It was a month later when I was introduced to Friendsgiving, in which I found another family. Countless people throughout this time have been a part of my story.

Some of the people I met through these next three years would go on to influence me to write this book without knowing. That first PowerPoint that was rejected had been accepted by these people. One of my bosses would often ask me the question, "What do you want to do in life?" While I was still silent, those conversations meant the world to me, knowing that this was it.

Another helped me with body confidence. He would go on to coach me for about a year, in which I hit body weights that I hadn't seen since I was in middle school. It was that same confidence that helped me follow through with this book—the countless hours in the gym, getting better one day at a time.

Now here we are, full circle in 2025, getting ready for another restart. Perhaps the scariest one of all, not knowing what will come next with this book. Giving up the stability of the Army for another change, good or bad, has yet to be determined.

But that's just it.

It was never about escaping home.

I was never about joining the Army.

It was never about becoming a Career Counselor.

It was never about becoming another author.

It was always about becoming the person that each goal required and the lessons learned from the people I met along the way.

WHY YOU SHOULD WANT TO CHANGE

If you are happy with your current life, then by all means, continue doing what you're doing. But if you are not satisfied with who you are or what you're doing, then there is no reason to stay the same. I'll ask you this question: *When was the last time a person asked you to help them become stressed, depressed, or filled with anxiety?*

The answer should be never.

But there are millions of people who ask: *How do I turn it all around? How can I make myself happy? How can I reduce stress? How do I overcome fear?* You must understand that life is hard. People love a comeback story, not the person who falls and never gets back up.

You see, it is easy to be depressed, it is easy to get into debt, it is easy to fail in life. *Anybody can fall, but not everyone chooses to rise back up. It takes accountability to accept that you have fallen. It takes courage to stand back up. It takes resilience to accept that you will fall but rise once again.*

Reflective Question:
- What will happen if you don't change?

CHOOSE TO LIVE

Every day you choose not to live, you are one step closer to death. You must choose to live every day of your life. Life is optional, but death is inevitable. Now, whether that is the case for today, tomorrow, or twenty years from now depends on whether you choose to live every day.

For death to come quickly, you must choose it, or you become chosen. For death to come slowly, you have chosen to live life but not to the fullest. *But for those who live every day, death is merely a friend who waits in the distance to be reunited at the end of a journey.*

Reflective Question:
- What life do you want to live?

WHY YOU FEEL LOST

You are probably not lost at all. Instead, I believe you are looking in the wrong direction. Whether you were misguided by yourself or others, though, is what you need to figure out. Perhaps you are waiting for a miracle to change that. *I will tell you that the miracle will not come because it has already happened.*

The miracle is and will always be you. Sometimes, we have to be lost before we are found.

Are you lost, or are you exactly where you are supposed to be?

WHO DO YOU WANT TO BE?

Whether you agree or disagree with some of my views, this is one of the more important lessons to take away. When you're down in life and no longer know what to do, you can't focus on who you are right now. Looking back at 2019, I was consumed with fear, hatred, loneliness, and anxiety. I had become someone I no longer recognized.

If I had focused on all those aspects, nothing in my life would have changed. Back then, I was a gamer. In a game, you must level up, set out on adventures, and decide who you are going to be. The problem was that, in this game, I didn't like the character I had made.

He wasn't brave, noble, or any other good thing. He was an NPC (non-player character) that had set dialogue, never leveled up, and lived the same day over and over again.

I realized I needed to create a new character.

When you are making that new character, you need to figure out what made the character bad to begin with. Otherwise, you will create the same character once again. So now you know the most essential part, which is what not to do. If your character is angry, you must choose different dialogue options. If you are stuck in the same place, you must pick new adventures. If you wish to level up, you must acquire new skills by taking actions you have never done before.

Instead of being the pessimistic person I was, I began to create the character I wanted to be. I focused on becoming what

I could be, rather than what I was. The first thing that had to go was my outlook on life. Instead of blaming the world for my problems, I looked for what it was trying to teach me. Instead of accepting negativity, I looked for what was going right in my life. I focused on achieving my personal improvement goals and on how I could help others. The biggest takeaway for me is knowing that *every day we wake up is an opportunity to become the person we want to be.*

THE PATH TO FOLLOW

On your journey to life, there will always be a path to take and a choice to be made. Some are simple: You can go left or right. Let's say the left path is wrong, and the correct path is right.

So, you go right, but if you are always correct, you will still find yourself stuck in a circle. The point is that you need to strike a balance between successes and failures. *If you do everything right, then you don't know what wrong looks like.*

Let's say next you go down the wrong path. It is straight, narrow, and has no end in sight. You can go down that path all your life. When you go down that wrong path, the important part to remember is that most of us don't get it right on the first try. Eventually, you will find that you're going to have to turn around and start over.

Reflective Question:
- What will you do the next time you find yourself on the wrong path?

THE OTHER PATH

I'm talking about the path that follows your heart. The one that people tell you is too risky to take. The one you are looking at right now, but perhaps you are too afraid of.

But it is the path you know you must take. It is yours to walk; it is your trail to tread. We both know the consequences for not taking that path, to be like everyone else when we know it isn't ours. We both know that you would have to continue to be who you are right now. Never taking a risk, never growing, and left with the question of "What if...?"

My friend, you cannot afford not to take that path. If you lose, you will learn something new that will lead to success later down the road. If you make it, then you will be glad you took the path. You must not betray your path; it is yours alone, and no one else can walk it. *If you stray from the path, then it will be lost forever, never to be traveled, and by doing so, you are denying other paths that would have been created from it.* You have an opportunity to change the world. Why not take that chance?

Reflective Question:
- What other paths will you deny by not taking yours?

WHAT IF...?

The next time you go to sleep, I want you to ask yourself, *What if...?*

What if...? will be different for everyone, but it usually starts with a daydream. The reason I want you to ask it when you're about to go to sleep is to see how badly you want it. If you fall asleep right away, you don't want it bad enough.

If it keeps you up until the morning, that's when you know it's time to wake up. I can't speak for everyone, but there is one thing that I do know. I can live with saying I tried, but I can't live with *What if...?* I couldn't continue to fall asleep knowing that I was living a life that wasn't mine. I hope, for your sake, that you start feeling the same way. If you don't, you will wake up one day and realize your nightmares have turned into reality.

That your dreams have been given up to somebody else who wanted them more than you. That they are living the life that was meant for you. Yes, every day, you wake up with the ability to change your mind. *What you cannot change every day is your life; that, my friend, has an expiration date.* You cannot wake up at sixty years old wanting to be an NFL player with no prior experience. The longer you wait, the less time you have. Don't let *What if...?* turn into *I should've.*

Reflective Question:
- What dream keeps you up at night?

WHY DID IT TAKE SO LONG TO WRITE THIS BOOK?

I have explained why I wrote the book, how I wrote it, and for whom it is intended. However, I have not yet discussed why it took me so long to sit down and write it. The book itself only took me a couple of months to finish. However, the idea had been in my head for well over a year.

Confidence caused the delay. I was still working on my self-confidence with my body at the gym. On most days, I didn't think about the music that was playing in my ears, but about my past. Half the time, it wasn't even music but motivational speeches. Those words repeated over two to three hours a day for a year straight, which is what started to build that courage. It is also what I played on my way to work. I listened to every word they said and asked myself: *Why not me?*

While confidence was the final push to get me out of my comfort zone, it was not the primary reason I held off on writing my book. *The book had always been in me, waiting to be written.* I knew I had a story that people needed to hear. I couldn't hold off any longer.

What took so long was that I knew, once I wrote the book, I could no longer go back. *It was the final death of my old character. There would be no more days of peace that were absent of responsibility.* There would be so many questions to answer, so many places to see, and new experiences to be had. Writing a book like this is accepting the responsibility not just for myself, but also for the world that needs to hear it.

I suppose that's how you know it's time to make a change in your life, when *you must say goodbye to that old friend to start living a new, more purposeful life.*

Reflective Question:
- What has to die for you to live?

CHAPTER 12

THE COST

You can start over, but are you willing to pay the price?

A FINAL DESTINATION

We are nearing the end of my story. But it is the beginning of yours. A book can only capture so many moments before it is overdone and repetitive. While I gave you the highlights of my journey, both good and bad, keep in mind I only showed you a couple of weeks of my life. While the timeline was over a decade, I only shared a brief snapshot.

For you, it was hours; for me, it was years. I hope this book does help you make that change you want in life, but everything comes at a price. So before you embark on that journey, I feel it would be irresponsible of me not to give you a final warning. You can choose to follow in my footsteps and find your way on the journey of self-discovery.

But the key word is self. At the same time, you will meet many people along the way. It is on you to make your best judgment to continue or remain in place. Perhaps you will meet someone worth more than the adventure you seek. But that wouldn't be much of a warning, though, would it?

The truth is that, despite talking about the dangers of isolation, it is where you will find yourself. There will be times when there are no voices to guide you and only your internal thoughts. If you fear being alone, then maybe this isn't the path for you. But then again, that is your call.

While I found many families on my path, I still walked alone. Each time I restarted my life, many of them faded away. It's the saddest part of the cycle that a lot of people don't talk about. While I still have contact information for each one, the days have turned into months without conversation. It's heartrending at times to realize you thought you had lifelong friends, but most were only meant to stay for a season.

While God is with you, he will not make your decisions. He will try to give you what you seek, but you must find it, as well. If you wage war with God, then that is when you will feel true loneliness, even when he is present.

While I encourage the journey of self-discovery, it is not a path for everyone. Many have tried, but I wonder how many ever reached the end? It's easy when you win, when you achieve the goal. But what happens when you do everything right and still don't end up where you wanted? After all, nothing is guaranteed in this life.

But what did I learn about life itself? What lesson came from all the isolation, the family, the suffering, the love, the betrayal, and the faith? I realized that each one has its place, and without any one of them, it wouldn't be much of a story. Here is my answer regarding the part of my story I have yet to reach.

Life is not suffering.

Life is the answer; suffering is just the price we pay to live it.

The scenario I can provide is the creation of life itself—the bond between a man and a woman that comes together to form life. But it comes at the price of sacrifice and suffering on both ends.

If he is a boy, then he must become a man, a provider. He must sacrifice his old ways of living to take care of his partner and his child. He must also become a protector, a lifelong duty until the child becomes a man or woman. Even when they become an adult, they will always be considered a child.

The female becomes more vulnerable than at any other time in her life. She suffers for the next nine months, housing another human being in her stomach. Then the most painful part of the process is the birth of a child, which literally tears the body apart. This process is so detrimental to the body that it will take weeks of recovery and often causes permanent changes.

Yet, when the baby is born, the tears of pain turn into tears of joy. Then, even if only momentarily, the pain disappears as the mother and father look into the eyes of their child for the first time. But the sacrifice and suffering have just begun.

What follows are tireless nights as the baby wakes every couple of hours. The baby can't walk, so it must be carried. It can't communicate; it only cries for what it wants or thinks it needs. It can't feed itself, and it can't change itself. It is 100 percent reliant on the father and mother—a sacrifice of their own time left on earth.

Yet before the baby is born, the love and internal bond are formed. Despite everything the baby does, it is still loved and watched over past adulthood.

Then the most miraculous thing happens, which I can't explain and have not yet felt myself. They look past the pain, sacrifice, and suffering. They decide to have another child. Life has to be the only answer; I see it no other way.

Looking back on my own path, it was filled with tragedy and long suffering. But even now, not knowing what comes next, I would go back to live this life once again.

WHAT TROPHY DO YOU WANT?

In life, you should always aim to be the prize. A prize is something you must earn through hard work, discipline, and being better at something than everyone else. You also need to figure out what kind of trophy you want to bring home. You mustn't bring home a participation trophy.

Everyone gets a participation trophy, so there is nothing special about it. If you relate this to a person, they have nothing to offer to the relationship. If everyone can get it, then the value is depreciated. You have to set yourself aside from others, but at the same time make yourself desirable.

An example of this is that you can get a prize that no one else has, but it may be because no one else wants it. When was the last time you saw someone proud of the amount of debt they owe?

You must also realize that while you want the best trophy, so does everyone else. Jealousy will always be a factor, and some will do everything they can to take your trophy away from you. When you are number one and your name is praised, you will gain enemies.

Reflective Question:
- Are you the prize or the participation trophy?

EVERY GIFT COMES WITH A CURSE

These gifts I'm referring to are something you were born with or acquired along the way in life. For each gift you acquire, you will also have a curse. Beauty comes with the curse of unwanted attention. The price of knowledge is sometimes knowing things you wish you didn't and having difficulty connecting with others.

Changing your body comes with the curse of perfection. *Changing your mind comes with the curse of remembering who you were.* The cost of living will always be time that you can never get back. The gift of patience is attained by waiting for something that may never happen. *The gift of giving joy often comes at the price of your own.*

> Reflective Question:
> - What are your gifts and the curses that follow them?

COST VS. WORTH

Do not mix up cost and worth; they are entirely different. The cost is what you pay for it, and the worth is based on the value it provides. Let's use the book *Think and Grow Rich* as an example. The book costs you anywhere from ten to fifteen dollars, and the time it takes you to read or listen to the material.

The value of the book, however, is worth billions of dollars. In this book, the experiences of some of the wealthiest people on the planet are shared. If you listen to seminars and motivational speeches, and pay close attention, you'll notice that many of them draw on stories and ideas from this book.

Jim Rohn wrote a very similar speech for *Think and Grow Rich* about cost and worth. He was worth $500 million, and it started with this book. Les Brown attended seminars by Jim Rohn. Eric

Thomas, who went from homelessness to becoming another famous motivational speaker, has also referenced this same book.

But if you run the stats, 100 million people have read this book, and the world population is around 8 billion. That means only about 1 percent of the world has read this book that can change their lives. Maybe it's just a coincidence that 1 percent of the population owns 50 percent of the wealth, or maybe it's not.

The top 1 percent have found something we haven't. As I'm starting to read more books, I can't help but notice that a single sentence can have the most significant impact. The question I leave with you is, if a book is worth a billion dollars, but only costs fifteen dollars, why does everyone not own a copy?

If something is given to you for free, then you are bound to lose it just as fast as you receive it.

Reflective Question:

- Are you willing to pay the cost to find the value? What is the "cost"?

THE AVERAGE LIFESPAN

Let's say the average lifespan is seventy-seven years. That is 924 months, 27,720 days, or 665,280 hours if you get the whole ride. Let's say you worked a nine-to-five job for five days a week from the age of twenty until sixty-two. That is 80,640 of your hours gone from your life.

If you sleep for, say, eight hours a night up until the day you die at seventy-seven, that is roughly 221,760 hours of your life. If it's six hours, then it is 166,320 hours. One hour to get ready in the morning, from the age of seven to seventy-seven, amounts to 25,200 hours. Adding another 25,200 hours for meals, plus some extra time for infant years, brings the total to 50,400 hours.

You also need to stay in shape, so let's say one hour a day, as well as five days a week, starting at sixteen, would be another 14,640 hours. So, without adding any variables and by doing the basics in life, we have 330,720 hours taken away by our daily responsibilities and human functions alone.

Half of our time in life doesn't even belong to us; one hour repeated every day is about 5 percent of our life. Think about this the next time you find yourself procrastinating or pushing something to the next day. Our time is limited, so we must make every second count.

Reflective Question:
- What will you do with the time you have left?

SACRIFICE THE PRESENT

The funny part about the present is that it is now in the past. This is why time is so valuable; there is no second chance, just heat-of-the-moment actions. You cannot prep for life, you cannot reason with it, but you can choose to live it. To do that, you must sacrifice the present to build a better future.

A million dollars is on most people's bucket list, and a majority will never see it. The short answer to why is that most people are not willing to pay the cost, which is time and financial discipline. To put it into perspective, it would take sixty years if you were to set aside $45.68 into an account daily, or $1,370.40 a month, to make a million dollars.

Now, unless you're born into a wealthy family, it probably won't happen. We then take off the first twenty years so you can get a job that allows you to save money. The price then is $68.50 every day until you're sixty once again. This is $2,055 a month, more than most people make after all their bills are paid. *The longer you wait and the less you sacrifice, the more you will owe in the future.*

OBSTACLES COME WITH REWARDS

Just like every gift comes with a curse, every obstacle you face has a reward. The more obstacles you face, the better the reward will be. Your best achievement didn't come because it was easy, but because it challenged you to be better. It is in that growth of wanting to be better that the reward hides.

Not all rewards come from wealth, recognition, or power. Some rewards are there to show you what is to come. Maybe you learned a skill that will turn into wealth. A story you wrote can turn into a stranger's redemption. Those who seek power are not always worthy of it. Power is for those who don't want it but have earned it; it's there when they need it.

The obstacles you face in life are there to reward the bold. To reward the ones who didn't see it as an obstacle, but as an opportunity to rise to the call. If you have faced no obstacles in life, then you have not tried hard enough. The reward is waiting to be earned—waiting for you. Take the challenge, accept responsibility, and claim your reward.

CHAPTER 13

THE FINAL TEST

Work in the darkness; shine in the light.

LET IT BE THE END OF A CHAPTER, NOT THE END OF THE BOOK

The first chapter of the book—how fitting that it is also a part of the end. What started as just a title will now be a story. It's the lesson that has echoed throughout the book but has yet to be explained. It's the ultimate choice you will have to make when life itself has become questionable.

Imagine you are reading a book—this book, to be exact. Maybe you had a life that makes mine look elementary. You're looking for the answer to life and death itself. That is the purpose of reading a story: You're looking for the connection, that one sentence that can turn your life around.

The more you read, the more entranced you become. At the beginning, you thought you were alone. But now you clearly see that everyone goes through their own tests in life. The author is at his most vulnerable place, giving you a small glimpse into Hell itself. Perhaps it's the same Hell you find yourself in now.

While you told yourself just one more page, now here you are deep into the book. You turn to the next page to find out how the narrator made it out alive. But the page is blank, which means it is the end of the chapter. You turn the next page to discover it is also blank. You begin to panic as you realize that this isn't the end of the chapter. It is the end of the book.

No hope, no redemption, no change, no second chance. All you are left with is emptiness.

When you end your story early, it doesn't just affect you. It affects everyone who needs to hear your story. You lost hope and therefore took it away from everyone else.

Let it be the end of a chapter, not the end of the book.

DEATH

I believe the purpose of death is to make us appreciate life. It's there to remind us that nothing is guaranteed. At any given moment, you can die, whether in one hundred years or five seconds. The timing is unknown. Given the unknown factor of death, it is our responsibility to be thankful for the time we are given.

The time you did or did not have is irrelevant, because some of us will die before even having a chance to live. For those who have gone through that experience, I do feel sorry for you. As someone who has never had a child, it is still a concept I don't fully understand. But sometimes one death can change many lives.

When I was on the verge of turning twenty, I received the news that my mother was dying, and I didn't confront the emotions I was feeling. The anger I felt for her, for not being able to get that second chance in life. The grief I felt for myself, for never being able to tell her that I was proud of her before she passed.

It wasn't until I found myself in a hospital that I finally understood the lesson of life and death. Although my mother's life was cut short, I was given a second chance. I focused on the wrong aspects of her death. Despite her leaving this world early, I was still given nineteen years to know her.

There are people out there who were never given parents. I had to learn not to focus on the death of my mother but on the time I was given with her. Although loved ones have passed, their memory still remains. Even if you never had a mother or a father, be proud in knowing that you are still here.

I know that it's a hard concept to understand at this moment. I'm not saying you shouldn't be sad; all emotions are meant to be had. *But remember, the more time you mourn someone's death, the closer yours becomes.* We have to look past the pain and turn it into something we can use to benefit others. Those who have experienced loss and still found peace in life are there to guide the next person through their suffering.

Reflective Question:
- What death has hurt you the most, and how are you doing?

WHY DO WE SUFFER?

Suffering is an inevitable step in finding your peace. *Suffering is not there to break us. It is there to show us what we are truly capable of.* When you are suffering, you are always presented with two options. You can allow suffering to define who you are, or you can allow the suffering to build you into what you could be.

Those who are defined by suffering are trapped by what happened to them. Those who were built by suffering took the pain and found a deeper meaning. If you take suffering at face value, then you will continue to suffer.

The trick for those who can endure the pain is that they don't focus on the pain itself. While everyone else sees pain, they find hope, drive, and compassion. They see that despite all the pain and suffering in the world, people continue to move forward.

Reflective Question:
- What is the purpose behind the pain?

THE DARKNESS

Most people shy away from the darkness. Their fears, insecurities, regrets, and unwanted feelings are caused by themselves or others. This is where all the work begins and where you find the answers to life's hardest questions. You do not learn much from the light; that is not where the lessons are meant to come from. That is the reward for when you work through the darkness.

I say you should *do as much as you can in the dark so that when you come to the light, you shine brighter than everyone else.* The hard part is that you must control the dark thoughts; otherwise, they will control you. *When you wake up in the morning, you put the darkness to sleep—because if you allow the darkness to put you to sleep, you may never wake up.*

Reflective Question:
- What did you learn on your darkest day?

THE PURPOSE OF LIGHT AND DARKNESS

Just like the hero and the villain, you cannot have one without the other. The purpose of the darkness is to test those who want to stand in the light. When we are born, we often have to be taught to be good people and not the other way around. Being in the darkness is not hard, because it is where we are born. The purpose is not to be consumed by it, but to learn from it.

The lessons you learn while in that darkness are what will define who you are. If you curse the world and everyone in it, then you will remain a puppet of the darkness. *For some, it's in their darkest moments when they will see the light for the very first time.* The funny thing about the darkness is that *wherever the light is, the darkness cannot go. When you learn that lesson, the world will seem just a little less dark.*

Reflective Question:
- What lessons did you learn from each side?

TWO WISHES

During the transition from the dark period to a new mindset, I made two wishes to the universe. The first was to be normal. This wish was made early on in life; even in my teenage years, it is something I sought. During that time, I was still trying to figure out who I was. I just wanted to be like everyone else. Nothing extreme—just having friends, starting a relationship, and making a family, to feel like I truly belonged somewhere.

My second wish was to be happy. Now, the funny part about the universe is that it knows what you want more than you do, which is why it never gave me my first wish of being normal. For me to be happy and to be normal would never work. Being normal is what everyone else was doing. Maybe I could trick myself into thinking it was for me. But that was precisely the mindset that got me here in the first place.

Sometimes, no matter how normal we want to be, the universe has different plans for us. Sometimes we are sent here with a purpose that cannot be ignored. *To stand out from the crowd, not to follow, but to make our own path and pass that on to someone else.* Now, for the happiness that was granted, however, everything comes at a price. Sometimes to be happy, you must suffer, and by doing so, figure out what makes you unhappy. From there, it's straightforward; you know what you don't want. You can now pursue what you believe would make you happy.

Reflective Question:
- Did you actually want your wishes to come true? Why or why not?

LOOK UP, NOT DOWN

We are born on the ground, we walk on the ground, and when we die, we are buried beneath the ground. When you speak to a mentor, you *look up* to them. When you fall, you *stand back up*. As you mature in life, you *grow up*. When you go up, you are rising to the challenge. When you start to look down, that is when you fall.

Perhaps that is why many are so fascinated with religion: the awe we feel when searching for something above ourselves; the love of flight or even the stars in the night sky; reaching for something we can't touch but want to chase.

Death is guaranteed and of the Earth; how appropriate, then, that we get buried down into the ground. Heaven is above the sky but only out of reach for those who don't believe.

Heaven is not guaranteed. It is earned by struggling down here on the ground first.

A NEW WISH

I wish I could tell you that everything is going to be okay.

But we both know that life will always come up with new challenges.

I wish that I didn't have to write *Answering the Hard Questions*.

That life could be easy for everyone, and no one would have to suffer.

I wish I could tell you that after reading this book, your life will get easier.

But it is only the start of a long, narrow pathway paved by obstacles.

I wish I could tell everyone that you will turn your life around.

But that is not my decision to make.

I wish you luck on your journey. I hope the weight of your burdens becomes lighter to carry. Maybe you don't believe in yourself, but I do.

CHAPTER 14

THE CLOSING

All good stories must come to an end. But yours is just beginning.

HOW THIS BOOK WAS MADE

Originally, I intended to write this book as an autobiography, telling my full story of those dark days. But about forty statements in, I realized that the book had begun to take a different direction. What started off as notes turned into a story. I then asked myself how I could make this different from all the other stories out there.

I had recently started reading a book called *The 48 Laws of Power*, which has many stories within the laws themselves. I wanted to mirror the structure of that book, since it directly related to my statements. I then used that to create a new direction: Every statement would prompt a question for myself or readers, incorporating some stories and metaphors. Then I broke it down into acts and ordered them based on the tone.

The acts were a good start to the book, but those later became chapters. Chapters allowed me to break down the categorization of my statements further. It also helped with the flow of the book. For example, the darkness and death were in the middle of the book. It was a hard act to read, and there wasn't much light. With chapters, I could have both buildup and breaks of inspiration in between.

The last change I added was the memoir portion. I leaned into self-help too much. It was then pointed out: *Why should they follow you if you haven't told the full story?* The long stories you see toward the front of each section are around ninety-five pages. I wrote those pages within ten days.

I'm glad it was something people called out; without the change, it would have ended my own story too soon. The other part was that it had too many questions, which then took away from the purpose of my own book: telling my story. Instead of giving you two to three questions per section, I limited it to one each, choosing only the best questions.

But overall, the theme of the book is to show people not to focus on all the negative things happening to them. It is a book that provides hope. But how can I continue to provide hope if every statement is negative? *If you want to change the world, then you need to do something the world hasn't seen yet.*

ONE DAY

Take the time to go outside and look at everything around you.

The conversation we are having could happen in a year, but the time will never be the same; they have both passed.

The air through the trees will never blow the same. The trees' leaves will fall and grow anew.

The waters will never have the same ripple as they do now.

The buildings will not stay the same even though they never move.

The sky will never be as perfect as it is right now.

The sun will never shine quite as bright.

Take it all in. One day, it will all be gone.

The opposite can also be said.

The pain and suffering you're experiencing will all be gone one day, too.

They are not a curse, but a luxury of life—reminders that we are alive, capable of feeling, and capable of healing.

THE GOLDEN TOUCH

Once there was man with a golden touch that could fix anyone. If they were sick, he touched them, and they became healthy. If they were injured, he healed them. If they were poor, he made them become rich. But the man had a problem: He could turn anything into gold except himself. In his eyes, this inability was a curse. He could help others freely but could never help himself.

So, one day he touched a fool so that he would become a wise man. He then asked him, "Why can't I make myself golden?"

The wise man then said, "You cannot be healed because *there is nothing wrong with you*. You were always what made the touch golden."

THE SPEECH

Fear is what keeps a lot of us from pursuing what we want to do in life. For some, it's the fear of failure; for others, it is the fear of judgment. I am here standing before you to let you know that it is possible to overcome them both. Fear is not our enemy; it's a friend asking us to take the next step. Failure is a teacher showing us what not to do.

What took me ten years to overcome is available for you in

THE DOOR

As I stand before you, I can tell you that I enjoy the person I am today. I look back at what I came from, and I am proud of the work I put into getting here. The door is different for all of us. No matter what type of door yours is, I want you to pause and think about who you are right now before proceeding.

That door represents an exit from your old life and the entrance for your new one. It doesn't matter whether it's a door at a job you hate, a door at a prison for the mistakes you made, or a door at the house of a friend you have outgrown.

At the end of the day, I will walk out my door a happy man. The question is: *Will you do the same?* If you don't like who you are, now is the chance to figure out who you want to be. Do not walk out that door as the same person you are right now.

THE END OF THE STORY

Here we are, finally at the end of the story. You have stayed for both the bad and the good, each one providing its purpose. You now know my darkest secrets and how my mind functions. But what you may not have pieced together was that this story has nothing to do with me and everything to do with you.

Some of you came here to find answers. Some of you came to see the real me—who I was and who I am. But the story had already been written years ago. *The story was always for you. To give you hope when there is none. To provide a light in your darkest night. I have changed my mind; the question is, when will you?*

THE QUESTIONS

YOUR STORY BEGINS HERE.

ASK YOURSELF HARD QUESTIONS

What is the hard question that you are avoiding asking yourself?

TELL YOUR STORY

Why haven't you told it yet?

Why haven't you told it yet?

THE MOST IMPORTANT LESSON
A PARENT CAN TEACH

What is something your parents would do that you didn't understand until later in life?

What dreams have you been silent on?

IT ONLY TAKES ONE QUESTION

What is the first question you need to ask yourself?

COMPLETE HONESTY

What is the truth you are hiding from?

WHY I CHOSE TO LIVE

Why do you choose to live?

Why do you choose to live?

WHY I WROTE THIS BOOK

If you were to write a book about your life, how would that book help others?

WHEN YOU HAVE NOTHING

If everything were taken from you, what would remain?

WHY DO YOU NEED TO BELIEVE IN SOMETHING?

What would happen if you believed in something greater than yourself?

WHAT IS STRONGER—FAITH OR HOPE?

Do you rely more on faith or hope, and how has that affected you so far?

DO YOU BELIEVE IN FREE WILL?

Do you believe you control your actions, and why?

Do you believe in perfection?

Do you believe in perfection?

MY BIGGEST STRUGGLES WITH FAITH

Do you avoid belief out of doubt, out of fear of being wrong, or something else?

YOU CAN MAKE YOURSELF DEPRESSED

What is your current mindset, and does it need to change?

WHAT DO YOU SAY TO YOURSELF?

Are you being hard on yourself or overly critical? What needs to change?

DO I REGRET SOME OF THE DECISIONS I MADE AT THAT TIME?

What did you learn from your regrets in life?

If you struggle with isolation, why are you afraid of being alone?

DO YOU ALWAYS NEED TO APPLY ALL THE LESSONS?

What set of beliefs would you die for?

IS MOTIVATION NECESSARY?

If you rely on being motivated, what happens when motivation
fades?

Maybe you tell everyone you're fine—but are you?

....

....

....

....

....

....

....

....

....

....

...........Maybe you tell everyone you're fine—but are you?...........

If you faced no obstacles in your life, what would you do?

WHAT IF I DON'T DESERVE WHAT I DESIRE?

What would it take for you to feel that you deserve your desires?

Who is the villain in your story?

Who is the villain in your story?

Do you need to take action or be patient, listen, and observe?

WHAT MAKES SOMEONE SUCCESSFUL?

Mindset versus action: Can one succeed without the other?

Is your grind producing the results you are looking for?

Who are the members of your council, and why have you chosen them?

BE PATIENT, LISTEN, AND OBSERVE

When do you need to remain silent, and when do you need to speak?

PROTECT YOUR DREAMS

Are you protecting your dreams? If so, how?

WHAT YOU DON'T ALWAYS NEED

What started as a disadvantage and turned into an advantage?

QUIT PREDICTING THE FUTURE

What biases have you developed through past experiences in your life?

Are you ready? Why or why not?

YOU WILL BE TESTED

If you fail the test, what will you do next?

If you fail the test, what will you do next?

When you failed previously in life, what was the progress you made?

IS FAILURE BAD?

How will your next attempt be different?

HOW MUCH DOES LUCK PLAY A FACTOR IN THE STORY?

How are you going to make the odds favor you?

What did you learn from your heartbreak that you still apply to relationships?

WHY MUST PEOPLE FALL?

What lessons have you learned from others' mistakes?

FEAR OF REJECTION

Did you continue to improve in the face of rejection, and if not, why?

HOW TO OVERCOME FEAR

What fear holds you back the most?

Which area do you struggle with the most, and why?

THE MOST IMPORTANT PERSON IN
YOUR LIFE SHOULD BE YOU

What are the consequences of not being the most important person in your life?

....

....

....

....

....

....

....

....

....

....

....

WHAT GOT ME THROUGH THE HARD YEARS

What have you used to survive that might now be holding you back?

MY BIGGEST STRUGGLE

What has been your biggest struggle in life?

What is the pattern in your cycles?

What is the pattern in your cycles?

What is keeping you from taking action and moving on?

FORGIVE BUT DO NOT FORGET

Who do you still need to forgive?

Who do you still need to forgive?

THE SANDSTORM

When was the last time you did something that made you uncomfortable?

What experience in life scares you the most?

What experience in life scares you the most?

What will you do if a piece no longer fits in your puzzle?

REMEMBER WHERE YOU CAME FROM

What will you do differently than those who came before you?

What will happen if you don't change?

CHOOSE TO LIVE

What life do you want to live?

What will you do the next time you find yourself on the wrong path?

What other paths will you deny by not taking yours?

WHAT IF...?

What dream keeps you up at night?

WHY DID IT TAKE SO LONG TO WRITE THIS BOOK?

What has to die for you to live?

WHAT TROPHY DO YOU WANT?

Are you the prize or the participation trophy?

Are you the prize or the participation trophy?

EVERY GIFT COMES WITH A CURSE

What are your gifts and the curses that follow them?

COST VS. WORTH

Are you willing to pay the cost to find the value? What is the "cost"?

THE AVERAGE LIFESPAN

What will you do with the time you have left?

What will be the reward/consequence for sacrificing now?

What will be the reward/consequence for sacrificing now?

OBSTACLES COME WITH REWARD

What reward you are looking for?

What reward you are looking for?

What death has hurt you the most, and how are you doing?

WHY DO WE SUFFER?

What is the purpose behind the pain?

What did you learn on your darkest day?

THE PURPOSE OF LIGHT AND DARKNESS

What lessons did you learn from each side?

Did you actually want your wishes to come true? Why or why not?